Hey, it's the condensed version, yo!

the anti-textbook of writing
(remixed)

{Some content by students, some content by others (OER) and some content by Sybil Priebe.}

DEDICATION

This book is dedicated to all the students. May you have teachers who are kind and compassionate and full of ideas to help you learn.

TABLE OF CONTENTS

Use Command-F to find topics if the hyperlinks, for some reason, don't work in the digital version of this book.

ATTRIBUTION AND OER REVISION STATEMENT
The Anti-Textbook of Writing, compiled by Sybil Priebe, is licensed under CC BY-NC-SA 4.0,[1] except where otherwise noted.

The Anti-Textbook of Writing retains some content from the original *Anti-Textbook* published in 2013 by Sybil Priebe under Copyright, but it's been remixed with other OER, plus – the best part – diverse student examples have been added! In addition, the genres unit was expanded to include Tweets and Texting and Poetry (etc.), an extended array of strategies will only be included in the Expanded Version, and a chunk on Ungrading was implemented, too, among other cool things.

Teachers should feel free to use whichever chapters work best for them and cut out the rest. Various formats of *The Anti-Textbook of Writing* can be found in this Google folder: bit.ly/NDSCS-Open-Folder. *The Anti-Textbook of Writing* is designed to be the blasphemous take on college writing. Proceed with caution.[2]

ACKNOWLEDGEMENTS
Cover image of Shakespeare: http://www.flickr.com/photos/tonynetone/2688212829/ by Tonynetone; CC-BY 2.0. It was modified by using the tools at Pixlr.com.

Thank you so very, very much to my past students for sharing their work.

+

ISBN: 9798784823847
Imprint: Independently published

---

[1] This license lets others remix, adapt, and build upon this work non-commercially, as long as they credit me and license their new creations under the identical terms.
[2] Hee hee hee.

Sarah Osment
@sm_osment

today i asked my class to come up with a pair of terms that share a denotative meaning but whose connotative meanings differ and one student offered BUTT DIAL and BOOTY CALL anyway that student's the professor now

8/27/18, 3:47 PM

---

[3] Denotative means dictionary meaning; connotative means the additional meaning BEYOND the dictionary definition.

Hi. Here are some semi-important pieces of information.

OPEN EDUCATIONAL RESOURCES

Open Educational Resources are teaching and learning materials that are available for free use by students and teachers everywhere. The move toward OERs has really taken off recently—financially to help students, the flexibility aids teachers, and all along they have been the catalyst for social justice, too. Open resources are easy to access and use and are continually updated and revised.

You're reading one right now!

FRAMEWORK FOR SUCCESS IN POSTSECONDARY WRITING[4]

The concept of "college readiness" is increasingly important in discussions about students' preparation for postsecondary education.

This Framework describes the rhetorical and twenty-first-century skills as well as habits of mind and experiences that are critical for college success. Based in current research in writing and writing pedagogy, the Framework was written and reviewed by two- and four-year college and high school writing faculty nationwide and is endorsed by the Council of Writing Program Administrators, the National Council of Teachers of English, and the National Writing Project.[5]

Habits of mind refers to ways of approaching learning that are both intellectual and practical and that will support students' success in a variety of fields and disciplines. The Framework identifies eight habits of mind essential for success in college writing:

- Curiosity – the desire to know more about the world.
- Openness – the willingness to consider new ways of being and thinking in the world.
- Engagement – a sense of investment and involvement in learning.
- Creativity – the ability to use novel approaches for generating, investigating, and representing ideas.
- Persistence – the ability to sustain interest in and attention to short- and long-term projects.
- Responsibility – the ability to take ownership of one's actions and understand the consequences of those actions for oneself and others.
- Flexibility – the ability to adapt to situations, expectations, or demands.
- Metacognition – the ability to reflect on one's own thinking as well as on the individual and cultural processes used to structure knowledge.

---

[4] *Framework for Success in Postsecondary Writing* (2011) by the Council of Writing Program Administrators (CWPA), the National Council of Teachers of English (NCTE), and the National Writing Project (NWP) is licensed under a *Creative Commons Attribution-NonCommercial NoDerivs 3.0 Unported License.*

[5] These same groups do not endorse this awesome textbook. But they might someday? However, the textbook still thinks it's cool with or without the endorsement.

The Framework then explains how teachers can foster these habits of mind through **writing, reading, and critical analysis experiences**. These experiences aim to develop students'

- Rhetorical knowledge – the ability to analyze and act on understandings of audiences, purposes, and contexts in creating and comprehending texts;
- Critical thinking – the ability to analyze a situation or text and make thoughtful decisions based on that analysis, through writing, reading, and research;
- Writing processes – multiple strategies to approach and undertake writing and research;
- Knowledge of conventions – the formal and informal guidelines that define what is considered to be correct and appropriate, or incorrect and inappropriate, in a piece of writing; and
- Ability to compose in multiple environments – from traditional pen and paper to electronic technologies.

ANTI-TEXTBOOK LAYOUT

What went into this anti-textbook? What are the roots? What did Sybil start with? What's anti* about this textbook?

*Why anti? This goes against what textbooks of writing have done to students - told them there are rules, that their writing is "poor" when really their backgrounds have brought a different language to them. Their socioeconomic status doesn't make their writing or other communication skills "poor," just different. Their race or ethnic background doesn't make their skills "poor," just different. Same for their abilities, mental and physical. Same for their gender.

Is it possible to create a textbook that is TRULY INCLUSIVE TO ALL? A book that rips apart colonialism?[6] Maybe not, but this book is sure as hell going to try. This textbook aims to be PRO-student, not against students in its language and explanations. It will not assume that students will plagiarize, it will not assume that students need to be ranked and sorted, and it will not assume students are white and rich.

Yes, textbook FOR students needs to be AGAINST the textbooks of the past.

The anti-textbook contents could be brief since textbooks of the past have been wordy and boring. The anti-textbook could be visual. It might break grammar, punctuation, and spelling rules. The textbook is still a book, sure, but it's aim is to be VERY DIFFERENT. It'll include different chapters like ones about ungrading or self-assessment, how there are no rules, "white people's language," and optional writing process tips. The practice bits get upgraded, too, because this book includes all kinds of genres – even the ones that aren't considered "academic" to some, like memes and tweets.

QUESTIONS, EXERCISES, AND ACTIVITIES OH MY

This may not be a "blasphemous element" of this book, but it's FULL of questions and exercises and activities that one might not find in other textbooks. Students might be required to just read and respond to the questions, they might have to complete all exercises, and/or some of the activities could be conducted in both face-to-face and online sections of a writing class. There's a lot of variety and decisions to be made!

---

[6] From *Wikipedia*: "Colonialism is a practice or policy of control by one people or power over other people or areas, often by establishing colonies and generally with the aim of economic dominance. In the process of colonization, colonizers may impose their religion, language, economics, and other cultural practices. The foreign administrators rule the territory in pursuit of their interests, seeking to benefit from the colonized region's people and resources."

ACCESSIBILITY AND INCLUSIVITY

Here are the specific measures that were taken to ensure inclusivity in this book's content AND how students can gain access to that inclusive content.

What this all means is the following:

ACCESS

- This book is accessible in both paper and digital formats. The digital is free; the paper format is available through Amazon and students only pay for the paper since the book is under a $0 royalty.
- The digital formats come in Google Doc, Microsoft Word, PDF for print, and PDF for screen-readers. These formats are all available at: <insert URL>
- The book may be printed in Large Print eventually.
- Audio chapters will be offered via the LMS or a Google folder.

INCLUSIVITY

- Most of the he/she pronouns have been flipped for they/them pronouns.
- "White-sounding" names have been replaced by more diverse ones.
- "Husband" or "wife" have been replaced by "partner."
- The majority of examples in this book, by students or otherwise, are **not** written by white, heterosexual, cisgender men.

abby
@AbigailMulholl1

Today the 1st grader I was watching
said that she didn't understand why
kindergarten got naps because it's the
easiest grade. She said that college kids
should have naps because they only
get like 3 hours of sleep a night.
Make her president

7

7 Tweet was deleted sometime around December 6, 2018.

"LOVE" LETTER.

Dear Students,

Sybil's message on Day 1 in her hybrid classes: "I'm a white woman with a narrow lens of what writing is and I've only really read white authors. I acknowledge this and will push my lens wider by reading your pieces. This is why I also don't feel it's necessary for me to assess your writing; you will all tell me what you're learning and how you're growing."

+

I'm going to let you in on a secret that you may or may not already know: there is no one "right" way to write. Sure, you should probably know a little bit about grammar and maybe you should spell some things correctly, but if you look around and read emails from bosses and books from famous authors, you'll see that even people with degrees don't put commas where they "should" be, so why should you bother your brain to memorize that stuff?

You simply need to practice. And be open to learning all the ways to communicate.

This book can't perfectly prepare you for every writing – or communicating – opportunity that will pop up in your life. But[8] it will try. You might have a fussy customer who is arguing with you over email… or a boss who wants a certain kind of "report" by Monday… or maybe you want to write a letter to a company expressing your own concerns; these are real world things that could occur, so this book attempts to prep you for that.

But books can't do everything. And it knows that. So, be open to learning outside of the book, of course. Remind yourself that the world is changing, and that you should probably change with it.

Please know you can allow yourself to learn whatever you want. And it doesn't start and stop in high school or college.

Take care of your bodies,
take care of your brains,
and take care of your heart.

Sincerely,
Sybil & this goofy book

---

[8] Ooh, look! Yikes! Starting a sentence with a conjunction is "bad," isn't it? (Na.)

- You are different from every student I have ever taught. You write your own way. You talk your own way. You see things your own way. You have a unique laugh. Your life experiences are something new to me and to those around you. Bring that uniqueness, creativity, and perspective to your writing and to class discussion. And respect the different opinions and experiences of those around you.

- You are a busy person. You probably have a job, play a sport, or participate in some kind of school activity. You might have a significant other who wants to spend a romantic evening with you every once in a while. You might have a boss or coworkers that put a lot of pressure on you at work. You have bills and more bills. You have friends and family who get sick from time to time. You have a life. I understand and respect the fact that you have lots of stuff going on right now, this week, or this month. Remember, you selected this course at this time in your life. You chose to take this course during the time it is offered. We are happy to have you here among us, and we know that we are probably not your first priority in life.

How to be good at talking
1. Polite greeting
2. Name
3. Relevant personal link
4. Manage expectations

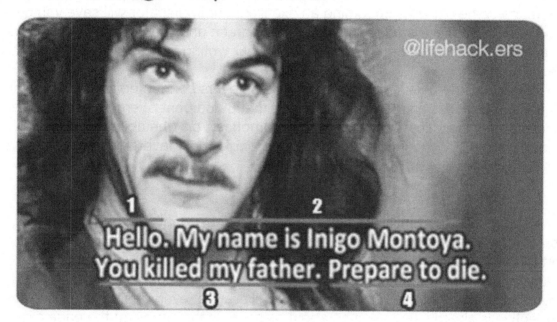

CHAPTER 1: INTRODUCTION

Hi. This chapter introduces you to stuff[10] you should know and think about before beginning to practice. It's kind of lengthy, BUT it's broken up by exercises, so maybe you read a little bit and then do some writing and then read some more bits and do some more writing, depending on what your teacher "assigns."

---

[9] Do you know where this reference comes from? Either way, what are the commonalities between talking and writing?
[10] This book sure uses the word "stuff" a lot. Is that "appropriate"?

YOU ARE A WRITER.

Obviously[11] you can write.[12] And in the age of Facebook and smartphones, you might be writing all the time, perhaps more often than speaking. Many students today are awash in text like no other generation before. You may have even performed so well in high school that you're deemed fully competent in college level writing and are now excused from taking a composition course.

So why spend yet more time and attention on writing skills? Research shows that deliberate practice—that is, close focus on improving one's skills—makes all the difference in how one performs. Revisiting the craft of writing—especially on the early end of college—will improve your writing much more than simply producing page after page in the same old way. Becoming an excellent communicator will save you a lot of time and hassle in your studies, advance your career, and promote better relationships and a higher quality of life off the job. Honing your writing is a good use of your scarce time.

Also consider this: a recent survey of employers conducted by the Association of American Colleges and Universities found that 89 percent of employers say that colleges and universities should place more emphasis on "the ability to effectively communicate orally and in writing." It was the single-most favored skill in this survey.

+

The most important belief[13] that a writing teacher can have about writing is, as Peter Elbow (a well-known teacher of writing) put it, that everyone can write. And at the heart of that belief is the assumption that everyone's experience and perspective is already worth writing about as soon they arrive in the classroom. To expand that belief beyond the classroom, we should generally believe that everyone's experience and perspective is already worth writing about as soon as they arrive at the page or screen. If this belief is essential for teachers of writing, it is even more so for the writers themselves.

QUESTIONS:

- Do you agree with Peter Elbow that "everyone can write"? Why or why not?
- Do you believe you are a writer? Why or why not?

---

[11] Oooh once again, Microsoft Word wants me to put a comma here, but I'm not going to!

[12] *Writing in College* by Amy Guptill is licensed under a Creative Commons Attribution-NonCommercial-ShareAlike 4.0 International License, except where otherwise noted.

[13] Snippet from = Brooks, Ronald Clark. "You Need My Credentials to be a Writer." *Bad Ideas About Writing*. Edited by Cheryl E. Ball and Drew M. Loewe. Morgantown, WV: West Virginia University Libraries, Digital Publishing Institute, 2017. CC-BY.

FIRST BATCH OF EXERCISES.

EXERCISE: WRITING TALLY.

Think of all the writing you do. Try to tally it all up – texting, email, to-do lists, homework. Estimate how many words you write weekly. Report that to your class/classmates. What are their estimates?

Now, ask yourself: How does taking in ALL those words affect who you are as a writer?

EXERCISE: WHO?

Create your own poem that has lines that start with "I am the one who..."
See example below:

```
I am friend of my demons
and the ghosts that tortures me.

I am the one who learnt
to enjoy loneliness
and the company of myself.

I am the one who listen music
read books
or watch movies
to find friends on the protagonists.

I am the one who walks alone in the beach
to see the waves
birds
feel the sand in my feet
and delights
with the world.

                        -axel marazzi
```

EXERCISE: QUESTIONS.

1. What is your favorite word? What is your least favorite word? What is your favorite swear word?
2. What movie/TV show/book character do you most identify with? Why?

---

[14] These activities may or may not be used in class to jumpstart our thoughts about writing and to get us writing in general. Maybe one activity will be assigned or none or all of them.

3. If the world suddenly turned into cartoon characters, who would you turn into? Why?

EXERCISE: ATTRIBUTES.

What are five (5) attributes that you inherited from your parents? If you aren't familiar with the word "attribute" look it up; it's common to refresh one's vocabulary from time to time and everyone – even teachers – look up words and their meanings!

EXERICSE: BORING INTRO.

Attempt to write a "boring" introduction of yourself.

EXERCISE: OLYMPICS.

Invent a new Olympic sport. There are many unusual Olympic sports, like skeleton (running and then sledding), biathlon (skiing plus shooting), and curling (using brooms to propel an object over ice). Make up a new sport that would be fun to watch and play.

EXERCISE: INVENTION.

Think about an invention that you'd like to have or make. Write about what this new device would do and why you'd like to use it.

EXERCISE: PARENTS.

Out of all the celebrities/famous people in the world, which two would you choose as your parents if you could? Why did you choose them?

EXERCISE: ANIMAL.

Invent a new animal – describe what it looks like, what it sounds like, how it moves, and what it eats. Is it scary or cuddly or something else altogether? Would it be a pet or live in the wild (or in a zoo)?

EXERCISE: HOLIDAY.

Invent a new holiday. What would this holiday celebrate? How would you celebrate it? Would there be any special food or symbols for your holiday?

RED PENS AND ELBOW PATCHES.

I have a memory[15] that really sticks out in my mind when I think of all the bad ideas about writing. I was at the dentist making small talk, and my dentist asked, "So what is it you teach at the university?" Squinting at the bright light above me, I responded, "I teach mostly first-year writing." "Uh oh!" he chuckled, looking back at the dental assistants behind him. "Better watch my grammar around you, huh?" He paused and said, thoughtfully, "You know, I should send my son to you. He can't spell to save his life!"

To be fair, these sorts of comments are made innocently enough and, anecdotally, they tend to happen a lot. The reason for this, I think, is because of a particularly bad idea about writing and writing instruction, one that surprisingly hasn't let up in the past 40 years: that first-year writing is a basic course in language, grammar, and syntax that prepares students for something called academic writing in the more "legitimate" courses in the university; and that its teachers consist primarily of error-correctors and behavior-modifiers armed with red pens and elbow patches. However, such an antiquated view of what first-year writing is and can be only scratches the surface of the kinds of learning possible in a writing classroom.

QUESTIONS:

- Is spelling "everything correctly" a sign of intelligence?
- What do students mean when they say: "I can't write well"?
- What do you think you should learn in a first year (of college) writing course?

[15] Snippet from = Branson, Tyler. "First-Year Composition Prepares Students for Academic Writing." *Bad Ideas About Writing*. Edited by Cheryl E. Ball and Drew M. Loewe. Morgantown, WV: West Virginia University Libraries, Digital Publishing Institute, 2017. CC-BY.

[...]

However, people in the field of composition have come to learn a lot about how writing works and how it is best taught in courses like first-year writing. Scholars have found that teaching grammar and mechanics does not improve student writing. There was a famous study of errors in Freshman Composition essays and found that "the rate of student error is not increasing precipitously but, in fact, has stayed stable for nearly 100 years." What they mean is that errors in writing are a fact of life. As writing teachers, the idea that errors are a fact of life has been quite helpful because it has allowed them to prioritize higher order issues in writing like argument, analysis, audience, purpose, and context. By having students focus more on argument and audience in their writing, the five-paragraph essay template becomes increasingly irrelevant because it doesn't resemble anything about how writing looks in the real world or what different audiences expect in different reading contexts. Writing isn't a set of formulas that you plug in to get different kinds of texts. Writing is a process of brainstorming, composing, revising, having your work read by others, and then revising again. This is a complex, in-depth process that goes way beyond correctness.

QUESTIONS:

- What do you think when you read this statement = "Scholars have found that teaching grammar and mechanics does not improve student writing"?
- What do students mean when they say they "don't know grammar"?
- Is writing "well" more than spelling and punctuation and grammar? How do you know?
- What do you know about the five-paragraph essay? Why do some think it's so darn important?
- What do you think of the statement: "What they mean is that errors in writing are a fact of life"?

WRITING IS SUBJECTIVE.

Let's start with this: writing is subjective. Let's also start with this tweet by Dan Martin:

"I try to teach students to let go of the notion that good writing has a universal definition or that anyone can define what good writing is or can be for every situation."
@danmartin_7

How can one claim that writing is subjective? Well, for one, no one can agree on ONE author or one book that is truly THE BEST of all time. Sure, people will argue that they can. Your high school English teachers might've adored X,Y, and Z. But that's their opinion. My favorite writers haven't been part of the mainstream. They are different. They have affected me in ways that I'll never quite comprehend. That's what makes them the best to me, and you probably like completely different authors and books, too. Where does young adult literature fit into all this? Where do graphic novels? See? It's subjective as hell!

What can we do, if writing is subjective and doesn't have PERFECT rules then? We just practice the genres we know. We give it our best shot. We just learn new things and practice them and then practice some more.

+

Sunday September 28, 2008[16]

On Ellen the other day, Kid Rock[17] made a few anti-iTunes statements which I found interesting. To paraphrase, he said people shouldn't have to pay the same for every song because some are worth more than others. He then used the example that pricing a garage band's song the same as a Bruce Springsteen song was ridiculous. Now, I can sorta see his point; however, who can decide that? I mean, it's so subjective. If I had my way, then, everything I think is crappy should be 49 cents and everything I think is awesome is 99 cents or more. Anyhow, I think the statements were made after he promoted his songs on a site that were free or something. Ellen said she agreed with him, but there was an awkward pause in her reply which leads me to think she agreed so he wouldn't bash an empty beer bottle over her head. Posted 9/28/2008 at 3:11 PM

+

---

[16] You may see old blog posts of Sybil's throughout the book. They are used to punctuate or emphasize the lesson in the chapter. They are licensed CC-BY.

[17] Yes, Ellen and Kid Rock are imperfect humans, but this blog post gets at the idea of subjectivity.

Wednesday May 23, 2007

David Eggers:[18]

- "I had great teachers. I had fantastic teachers, all the way through school. At least I was encouraged by them. I never had an English teacher who said no you've got to fit in this category and you've got to write this way."

- "I think it's always the great killer of any potential writer if an adult says no it's got to be this way, this is how it's done, five paragraphs, topic sentence, introduction, conclusion, whatever. I think that the teachers we learn a lot from really untether their students and let them go at it from whatever angle they feel they should. The last thing you want to do is impose any kind of paralysis before they get started."

- "I think that once students know you're serious and once you're setting an example where you're being honest and you're saying you will not be judged, you will not be chastised, there's no wrong, that's where you get the most incredible writing. We've gotten it out of every conceivable student. [...]"

{from his keynote at an arts and humanities summit at NDSU}

Posted 5/23/2007

Tuesday February 5, 2008

Can you truly love something/someone if you've never hated something/someone? Can you know a "bad" person if you've never known a "good" person? How do we know when life is being fair, if we've never known "unfair" circumstances? If my sister claims I am so lucky, she must know what it is like to be unlucky? Right? I consider myself "open-minded," but can I describe what it is like to be "close-minded"? The first question was part of the BIG topic in today's Creative Writing class. A few students claimed to not/never having hated anyone (as our poem topic asked them to do: Write a poem from the P.O.V. of someone you "strongly dislike, and are morally or physically repelled by."), and I didn't believe them. Am I that cynical or are they "full of it"?

[...]

Posted 2/5/2008 at 4:11 PM

QUESTIONS:

- What do you think of Kid Rock's argument made in the first blog entry?
- Is David Eggers right about the greatest killer of student writing?
- Try to answer the questions in the last blog entry.

---

[18] This is from his keynote at an arts and humanities summit at NDSU.

THE "WHITE PEOPLE" LANGUAGE.

> *I've[19] been fumbling around w/this idea for a while, & I dunno if I'll say it correctly, yet I also know I'm not the first to say it: when we tell Ss to write "professionally" or use "appropriate language/grammar/spelling," we're saying, "You should sound like a white person." T/F?*

+

People[20] consistently lament that kids today can't speak properly or that people coming to this country need to learn to write correctly. These lamentations are based on the notion that there is a single correct way of speaking and writing. Currently, the general sentiment is that people should just learn to speak and write proper English. This understanding of writing is rooted called current traditional rhetoric, which focuses on a prescriptive and formulaic way of teaching writing that assumes there is only one way to write (or speak) something for it to be correct. However, over the past several decades, scholars in writing studies have examined the ways in which writing has a close dialectical relationship with identity, style genre, and culture. In other words, the rules for writing shift with the people and the community involved as well as the purpose and type of writing.

This means that while minority students and lower-class students are ostensibly being given greater access to education, careers, and other facets of society they had been previously barred from, they are still facing serious barriers that their upper-class white counterparts do not, particularly in terms of culture, language, and literacy.[21]

The way that we conceptualize language is not just detrimental to minorities; it also devalues the identities that working- and lower-class people bring to communicative situations, including the classroom. Lynn Z. Bloom writes that "Freshman Composition is an unabashedly middle-class enterprise." She argues that one of the reasons composition is required for all students is because it promulgates middle-class values and ways of thinking. These values in the writing classroom are embodied in everything from the notion of property, which undergirds the way that plagiarism and intellectual property are treated, to formality of language and rhetorical choices that are encouraged in papers. Indeed, the way many instructors teach writing, plagiarism, citation, and word choice in papers is not in and of itself good but rather is the socially accepted way of interacting with text as defined by the middle class. Mike Rose and Irvin Peckham write about the tension of middleclass values on working-class students and the cognitive dissonance and struggles with identity that come with imposing such values in writing under the guise of correctness. The idea that there is

---

[19] Sybil's Tweet[19] from February 3, 2021.
[20] Snippet from = Pattanayak, Anjali. "There is One Correct Way of Writing and Speaking." *Bad Ideas About Writing*. Edited by Cheryl E. Ball and Drew M. Loewe. Morgantown, WV: West Virginia University Libraries, Digital Publishing Institute, 2017. CC-BY.
[21] This is why the theory of ungrading is so important in a writing classroom; teachers are not able to understand the efforts of all students, no matter their backgrounds. This is why students should assess their learning.

one correct way of writing devalues the writing, thoughts, intelligence, and identities of people from lower-class backgrounds.

In order to value the diversity of communication and identities that exist in the U.S., we need to start teaching and envisioning writing as a cultural and social activity. We need a more nuanced view of writing in society that encourages everyone to adapt to their audiences and contexts rather than placing an undue burden on those who do not fit the mold of standard English. One strategy for teaching academic English without devaluing a writer's identity is code-switching, a concept already taught in schools with significant minority populations as a way of empowering young people. While instruction in code-switching is valuable because it teaches students that they can adopt different linguistic choices to appeal to different audiences, it is deeply problematic that the impetus is still placed on minority students with non-standard dialects to adapt. While code-switching is meant to empower people, it is still rooted in the mentality that there is one correct way of writing, because even as code-switching teaches an incredibly nuanced way of thinking about writing, it is still being taught in the context of preparing writers to deal with a society that will use errors in speaking as evidence that they are lesser. As a result, it is a less-than ideal solution because it plays into—rather than undermines—the racism of academic English.

+

When we focus on the ways that African American Language and Standard American English are different,[22] communicators are able to better understand, acquire, and switch between both, and society is more capable of recognizing the validity of the language and its users. Conflating the two into one linguistic variety is confusing at best and damaging at worst. We need to understand and explain African American Language and Standard American English as different languages, each with its own set of grammatical, phonological, and morphological rules (even though they share a lexicon or vocabulary).

In the writing classroom, teachers can help students navigate Standard American English expectations while not suggesting a linguistic hierarchy. By speaking about language choices in terms of difference rather than deficiency and in relation to academic and nonacademic conventions, we can value both (or any) languages. Delpit suggests validating students by welcoming their home languages—and, therefore, their cultures and identities—into the classroom so they feel respected and might be more willing to add Standard American English to their linguistic repertoires. If students understand that different audiences and contexts expect different language choices and that African American Language is different from Standard American English but that neither is better or worse than the other, then they are better able to accept and use both proficiently.

---

[22] Cunningham, Jennifer M. "African American Language is Not Good English." *Bad Ideas About Writing*. This resource is licensed CC-BY.

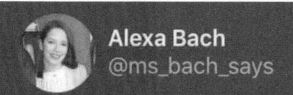

Alexa Bach
@ms_bach_says

PSA. Your students saying "ain't", "finna", etc. are cultural. Instead of "correcting" them, talk to them about code switching and how amazingly SMART they are for being able to codeswitch between the two. Valuing your students' identities means valuing the way they speak.[23]

QUESTIONS:

- Have you ever thought of the connection between racism and language? Why or why not?
- How many authors have you read who are not white?
- Have you ever thought of the connection between classism and language? Why or why not?
- How many authors have you read who come from lower income backgrounds?
- Have you ever thought of the connection between sexism and language? Why or why not?
- How many authors have you read who identify as women?
- What is code-switching?

---

[23] Tweeted July 25, 2018.

YOUR VOICE.

Sandra Cisneros[24] explains, "As a writer, I continue to analyze and reflect on the power words have over me." Cisneros's statement may resonate with emerging writers in classrooms, outside of classrooms, and spaces of their own making to write and create with language. Writers affirm their lives and empower the lives of others who connect with their words and concepts. The first-person point of view is an essential marker in the making of meaning for both the writer and reader and need not be abandoned nor silenced. Even if the self is briefly mentioned and noted in one's written deliberations, its use will suffice in making oneself known and present in the discussion of ideas, concepts, and perspectives. One learns about oneself as one writes and by asserting the self. Indeed, words and literacies carve the identities of writers who are influenced by the societies they inhabit and the subjects they study. In essence, words empower and define us as Cisneros observes.

Some writers across the disciplines, which include the arts, education, engineering, mathematics, technology, and sciences, attempt in various cloaked forms to remove their sense of self as they write under the assumption that writing must be as universal as possible. Unfortunately, this means less personality and presence. This is done in detrimental forms if the writer fails to acknowledge purpose, actions, and influences to an audience. Furthermore, writers and thinkers are connected to their subjects and arguments, which they deem worthy of explanation or description. As such, writers learn about themselves through their writing and the interconnectedness to thought and argument. In fact, writers give authority and credibility to experience through their expertise and in structure and argument. The reader entrusts the writer's self not only by the levels of expertise for having done the labor and research, but also by the valuable experiences drawn from analysis. In short, it is a false idea to eliminate one's first-person point of view in writing, rather than supporting the writer's personal and communicative voice on the print and digital page.

+++

It's worth considering[25] how writers first get chastised and come to believe they must leave themselves out of their writing in the first place. When they are just beginning to experiment with language, most of the writing they are asked to produce draws from personal experience: They write about their friends, families, and pets. Personal narrative abounds and overflows within their lines of writing on the page or on the monitor screen of their computer or device. Their writing revolves around who they are and what matters and happens to them.

---

[24] Snippet from = Rodriquez, Rodrigo Joseph. "Leave Yourself Out of Your Writing." *Bad Ideas About Writing*. Edited by Cheryl E. Ball and Drew M. Loewe. Morgantown, WV: West Virginia University Libraries, Digital Publishing Institute, 2017. CC-BY.

[25] Snippet from = Parker, Kimberly. "Response: Never Use 'I'." Response to: Rodriquez, Rodrigo Joseph. "Leave Yourself Out of Your Writing." *Bad Ideas About Writing*. Edited by Cheryl E. Ball and Drew M. Loewe. Morgantown, WV: West Virginia University Libraries, Digital Publishing Institute, 2017. CC-BY.

GUIDELINES FOR CREATING YOUR OWN VOICE[26]

It's one thing to have a voice that isn't used in your "professional life," it's quite another thing to figure out what you will sound like in communicating in the workplace and how that translates to paper/screen.

I mean… the real question is: How does one mesh their unique style of language with professionalism when they write for or in the workplace? Most teachers of writing would appreciate any number of combinations of individuality and technicality. And in the workplace, HOPEFULLY,[27] you will be able to observe the stylistic convention of your profession and your employer's organization, while simultaneously expressing your individuality, make reading easy for your audience and impacting them while they are reading.

Consider the following guidelines in light of the way they will affect your readers' view of your communication's individuality, usability/technicality, and persuasiveness. Based on what readers see, they draw conclusions about you and your attitudes that can enhance or distract from the persuasiveness of your communications.

GUIDELINE A: HOW MUCH DISTANCE?

How much "distance" do your readers expect you to establish? In personal style, you appear close to your readers because you use personal pronouns and address readers directly. How conversational the piece is may also convey this message. In your "workplace style" you might distance yourself from your readers by avoiding personal pronouns. The style you choose depends on the purpose of the writing and the audience.

GUIDELINE B: CULTURAL BACKGROUND

In the United States and Europe, employees often use an informal voice and address their readers by their first names. In Japan, writers commonly use a formal style and address their readers by their titles and last names. If a U.S. writer used a familiar, informal voice in a letter, memo, or e-mail, Japanese readers might feel that the writer has not properly respected them. On the other hand, Japanese writers may seem distant and difficult to relate to if they use the formality that is common in their own cultures when writing to U.S. readers. In either case, if the readers judge that the writer hasn't taken the trouble to learn about or doesn't care about their culture they may be offended. Directness is another aspect of voice. When writing to people in other cultures, try to learn and use the voice that is customary there. If possible, ask for advice from people who are from your reader's culture or who are knowledgeable about it.

GUIDELINE C: ETHICS GUIDELINE – AVOID STEREOTYPES!

---

[26] "Professional and Technical Writing/Rhetoric/Author/Style." *Wikibooks, The Free Textbook Project.* 8 May 2017, 01:04 UTC. 10 Oct 2019, 17:39 <https://en.wikibooks.org/w/index.php?title=Professional_and_Technical_Writing/Rhetoric/Author/Style&oldid=3215241>. Licensed CC-BY-SA.

[27] Truly, I hope you are all going to be able to be yourselves in the workplace, but that might not happen (bummer), so let's prepare for if that doesn't happen easily…

Stereotypes are very deeply embedded in many cultures. Most of us are prone to use them occasionally especially when conversing informally. As a result, when we use more colloquial and conversational language to develop our distinctive voice for our workplace writing, we may inadvertently employ stereotypes. Unfortunately, even inadvertent uses of stereotypes have serious consequences for individuals and groups. People who are viewed in terms of stereotypes lose their ability to be treated as individual human beings. If they belong to a group that is unfavorably stereotyped, they may find it nearly impossible to get others to take their talents, ideas, and feelings seriously. The range of groups disadvantaged by stereotyping is quite extensive. People can be stereotyped because of their race, religion, age, gender, sexual orientation, weight, physical handicap, occupation, and ethnicity. In some workplaces, manual laborers, union members, clerical workers, and others are the victims of stereotyping by people in white-collar positions.

There is absolutely no tolerance for stereotypes in professional writing. Anything you write will be worthless to most audiences if you include any type of stereotypes. Using stereotypes, even accidentally, will seriously damage your reputation with your readers and may even cause your professional relationship to end. So, be very aware of any stereotypes that may exist especially when writing cross-culturally.

QUESTIONS:
- Are you writing cross-culturally in this classroom?
- What kinds of writing do you think you'll do in your future workplace?

HOLES IN DIVERSITY

Once one figures out their voice – in an academic setting or not – they can start to understand the necessity of employing that voice to tell their story. This book wants to encourage ALL humans to write, whether the writing is published or unpublished. One should note, however, that some stories are not as prominent in the "literature industry" and that makes them all the more valued to be told. Here are some examples:

- People of color, especially women of color
  - Examples: Roxane Gay, Maya Angelou, Toni Morrison, Alice Walker
- First Nations / First Peoples / Indigenous Peoples
  - Example: Louise Erdrich[28]
- Immigrants
  - Examples: Junot Díaz, Bharati Mukherjee, Jamaica Kincaid
- Humans who are LGBTQIA or pansexual or asexual or aromantic
  - Examples: David Sedaris, Augusten Burroughs, James Baldwin
- Humans with disabilities
  - Example: Octavia E. Butler
- Humans of size, a.k.a humans who are fat
  - Examples: Aubrey Gordan, Jess Baker

In particular, these types of stories seem to be missing from literature:

- Stories where one's skin color isn't the guiding factor of the plot
- Stories where the fact that characters are lesbians, or gay, or bisexual, or transgender or queer or intersex or asexual isn't the main topic of discussion
  - Example: the TV show, *Schitt's Creek*
- Stories about people with disabilities where the disability isn't the character's main "problem"
- Stories about fat people where intentional weight loss (IWL) isn't in the plot at all

QUESTIONS:

<insert questions here created by students>

---

[28] She has ties to the Wahpeton, ND area!

AUDIENCE.

No writing happens in a vacuum.[29] Writing, as a communicative activity, is made for an audience of readers. In practice, how readers interpret writing has far less to do with passive decoding or reception of a message developed by someone else. Reading is itself a constructive act—quite literally, reading is meaning making. From the perspective of the reader, then, being a part of an audience has power. Much of that power lies in the ways readers infer an author's voice into a text.

Suppose, for example, that you receive a love letter. You would likely interpret this letter differently depending on what you know about its author. If the love letter comes from your partner, you might cobble together memories of the author's familiar expressions, knowledge of the author's manners of language use, and even particular moments in the history of your relationship that imbue your reading of the letter with what you think the author's motives are. On the other hand, if your love letter is written by a secret admirer, you might find the whole notion of this letter awkward, flattering, intriguing, or intrusive. With this unknown author, you have less to go on to determine what the letter means, and with the knowledge you're lacking, the author's voice is distant, even inappropriate.

FAQ WHEN THINKING ABOUT AUDIENCE[30]

- Who is the actual audience for this piece of writing and how do you know?
- Who is the invoked audience for this piece of writing and where do you see evidence for this in the text?
- What knowledge, beliefs, and positions does the audience bring to the subject?
- What does the audience know or not know about the subject?
- What does the audience need or expect from the writer and the writing?
- When, where, and how will the audience encounter the piece of writing and how has the text—and its content—responded to this?
- What roles or personas (e.g., insider/outsider or expert/novice) does the writer create for the audience? Where are these personas presented in the piece of writing and why?
- How should/has the audience influenced the development of the piece of writing?

QUESTIONS:

- Will your voice – when writing – change with different audiences? How so?
- What is the difference between writing in and for the workplace and writing for audiences outside of your workplace?

---

[29] Snippet from = Thomas, Patrick. "Writers Must Develop a Strong, Original Voice." ." *Bad Ideas About Writing*. Edited by Cheryl E. Ball and Drew M. Loewe. Morgantown, WV: West Virginia University Libraries, Digital Publishing Institute, 2017. CC-BY.

[30] Questions taken from a longer piece by: Jory, Justin. "A Word About Audience." *Open English at Salt Lake Community College*. 01 Aug 2016. https://openenglishatslcc.pressbooks.com/chapter/audience/ Open English @ SLCC by SLCC English Department is licensed under CC-BY-NC, except where otherwise noted.

"A LESSON IN AUDIENCE"

DESCRIPTION OF WHAT I WOULD LIKE TO DO AS A CAREER.
AUDIENCE: 20-SOMETHINGS.
While I do love teaching and will have my master's degree this May in English Composition, I think I may want to try out Journalism as a part-time endeavor. Right now, I am: teaching three classes of English Composition 120 at NDSU, teaching two night classes at Aaker's College, and working as the Opinion Editor of NDSU's school newspaper, *The Spectrum*. Working and writing at The Spectrum has sparked a different type of writing in me. I would like to continue to teach, but I would also love to work for a magazine or newspaper as an Opinion Columnist, Fashion Columnist, or Features Columnist. Either one of these positions, I think, would really open up the side of my head that isn't use in academic writing. Journalist writing can be more playful, and I have many more readers of this type of writing than I will, say, for my sixty-page thesis paper.

DESCRIPTION OF WHAT I WOULD LIKE TO DO AS A CAREER.
AUDIENCE: KIDS AROUND THE AGE OF 10.
Right now, I am a teacher. I think I will always be a teacher, but I would like to write for a magazine or newspaper. Have you read a newspaper or magazine before? I would like to write words for something like that. I could write about where to go shopping for pink pants. I could write about movies like *The Incredibles* or *Shrek*. They are both almost the same because they deal with words. One kind is on paper, and the other kind is by helping people talk better and write bigger words.

DESCRIPTION OF WHAT I WOULD LIKE TO DO AS A CAREER.
AUDIENCE: MY GRANDPARENTS.
As you know, teachers don't make too much these days. If I were to teach in Minnesota, I think I could make a decent living, but I do like living in Fargo. If I stay in North Dakota or end up at a lower-paying school in the lakes area of Minnesota, I think I would like to find a part-time job as a journalist for a small newspaper or local magazine. I really enjoy being the Opinion Editor of *The Spectrum* this last year at NDSU, so I have some experience being a journalist. Since I wrote for the Opinion page, I would probably do that again, but I would be open to working on a Features story or being a Fashion Guru as well. Writing for a newspaper or magazine while I teach will expand my writing capabilities while also bringing in extra money too.

QUESTIONS:

- What are the differences between the three paragraphs above?

SECOND BATCH OF EXERCISES

EXERCISE: YOUR VOICE.

Find a piece of writing by someone, anyone. Then translate that paragraph (or dialogue or whatever it is) into YOUR VOICE. This may be tough but ask yourself how YOU would say the things in the piece by this other person. What words would you use instead? What words need to be added or deleted? Is the tone the kind of tone you like? How can that be changed to sound more like YOU?

EXERCISE: REMAKE "A LESSON IN AUDIENCE."

Return to the "Lesson in Audience" piece and recreate those three paragraphs with a different description/theme and different audiences (unless you'd like to use those same ones).

EXERCISE: STUDENT'S INDIVIDUAL CULTURE.

Teachers need to know as much as possible about their students to teach them well, including how they learn and the pace of that learning, multiple intelligences, personal qualities such as personality, temperament and motivation, personal interests, potential disabilities, health, family circumstances, and language preference.

In a paragraph, answer these questions:
- How do you learn best? What is the typical pace of your learning?
- When it comes to multiple intelligences,[31] which ones do you gravitate to and why? (Google this term if you have not heard of it.)
- How would you describe your personality, temperament, and motivation?
- What are a few of your personal interests?

In another paragraph, answer these questions:
- What do you have the desire to learn? Why?
- What is a challenge for you when it comes to getting an education? Why?
- What would be a challenge for you in this particular class?
- What would a risk look like for you?
- Are you willing to challenge the status quo?

---

[31] You may be more than one!

IT'S OKAY TO FAIL.

In fact, knowing what I know about learning to write[32] (as a writer and a writing teacher myself), I would argue that it is impossible for one to develop anything approaching a good writing ability without years—decades, probably—of repeated failure. We aren't born pen in hand, fully primed to write sonnets or political treatises as soon as we get a grip on those fine motor skills. Writing is learned slowly, over a long period of time, and with much difficulty, and anybody who says otherwise is lying or delusional or both.

What should be clear is that failure is a significant part of the entire scene of learning, an assertion that, again, is borne out by widely respected research. Malcolm Gladwell isn't wrong when he insists upon the 10,000-hour rule, which, in suggesting that it takes 10,000 hours to truly master anything (shooting free-throws, playing an instrument), implicitly builds in a generous rate of failure. It's true that writing is not stable in the way that chess is stable, but the broad message of Gladwell's limited theory—that to excel at anything takes a tremendous amount of practice and persistence— easily aligns with prevailing thought on what is central to development in writing: Writing is difficult and complex, and development is not linear.[33]

Failure is integral to learning and development, more so than external markers of achievement or success. An avoidance of failure in learning, or in writing, or in industry or parenting or any other human/community endeavor, represents an absence of creativity and an abundance of predictability, little to no risk, and perhaps even harmful or counter-productive thinking.

Instead, teachers, scholars, mentors, and anybody involved in the conversation about writing development should be taking concrete steps toward normalizing failure.

Writing is not a list of dos and don'ts, nor is success in writing a universally acknowledged ideal. Writing is about risk and wonder and a compulsion to make something known. Failure—and a willingness to fail often in large, obvious ways—should always be an option.

QUESTIONS:

- When have you failed at something? Did you learn from it?
- How do you feel about failing at writing in order to improve?
- Do you think it takes 10,000 hours to master something? Please give an example in your response.

---

[32] Snippet from = Carr, Allison D. "Failure Is Not An Option." *Bad Ideas About Writing*. Edited by Cheryl E. Ball and Drew M. Loewe. Morgantown, WV: West Virginia University Libraries, Digital Publishing Institute, 2017. CC-BY.
[33] This is why teaching students to follow the steps of the writing process perfectly is not ideal.

THERE ARE NO RULES.

Wisdom about writing[34]—as a product and as a process—is often expressed as hard and fast rules. Always begin an essay with a catchy hook. Never use the passive voice. Always make your writing flow. Always make a detailed outline before you start to write. Never edit as you draft.

+

In his article,[35] "The Phenomenology of Error," writing scholar Joseph Williams lists this history of fierce tirades against poor grammar and writing, but he also demonstrates that many "rules of grammar lack practical force." Williams takes a clever approach to make his point. He repeatedly shows that people, including some famous writers who express strong views about specific writing errors, fail to notice such errors in their own writing. Williams states that we often do not see errors unless we look for them, and he makes this assertion directly about the way teachers read and criticize their own students' writing. To further emphasize this point, Williams embeds 100 such errors in his own article and asks readers, mostly English teachers, how many they saw; doubtless, few noticed the vast majority of them. As readers, we tend to see errors where we want to, and we ignore errors where we do not expect to find them (such as a published article about writing!). Williams ultimately asks this: If an error is on the page but no one sees it, is it really an error? Does it matter?

QUESTIONS:

- Are there rules to writing?
  - Start with the list in the second paragraph:
    - Can you write a good essay without a catchy hook at the beginning?
    - Can good writing be done in passive voice?
    - Do some good writers have choppy writing, the kind that doesn't flow?
    - Do you have to outline everything you are about to write?
    - Can you edit as you write, and everything will turn out okay?
- What are the rules to writing that you've been taught? Take time to rethink why those rules exist. Are they legit rules? Are they myths? Are they just ways to get people to write "one correct way"[36] that doesn't really exist?

---

[34] Snippet from = Dufour, Monique and Jennifer Ahern-Dodson. "Good Writers Always Follow My Rules." *Bad Ideas About Writing.* Edited by Cheryl E. Ball and Drew M. Loewe. Morgantown, WV: West Virginia University Libraries, Digital Publishing Institute, 2017. CC-BY.

[35] Snippet from = Warnock, Scott. "Texting Ruins Students' Grammar Skills." Bad Ideas About Writing. This resource is licensed CC-BY.

[36] See the chapter on "White People Language" for more on this.

THE OUTLINE RULE[37]

Many undergraduate writers have been taught that they must create a detailed outline for a research paper before they begin writing. And they are often told that a first draft of a research paper must be presented in polished, error-free prose, and that the draft must be complete, from beginning to end. In fact, we know many teachers who refuse outright to read messy or incomplete works-in-progress. So, students put extensive effort into planning just how the essay will proceed and what it will say before they write. Of course, outlining can be a powerful conceptual and organizational tool. However, when writers believe that they must outline first, they often lock themselves into the ideas as expressed on the outline, rather than allowing their ideas to develop and change as they work.

THE CATCHY HOOK RULE[38]

Catchy hooks such as vivid anecdotes can be used to excellent effect, if they meet the needs of the text and the circumstances. A writer can try it out and see what happens. What effect does it have on the text? Does it meet the audience's and context's needs (i.e., the rhetorical situation[39])? Does it contribute to expressing what the writer is trying to say? How do real readers respond? In this way, writers can experiment with techniques, deliberate about their implications, and make judgments about the best course of action among their options. And, most importantly, writers focus their goals and purposes, rather than on the rote adherence to rules, which is more meaningful, and more fun.

QUESTIONS:

- Could an introduction that is "boring" work? Wait, what is a "boring" introduction?

---

[37] Snippet from = Dufour, Monique and Jennifer Ahern-Dodson. "Good Writers Always Follow My Rules." *Bad Ideas About Writing*. Edited by Cheryl E. Ball and Drew M. Loewe. Morgantown, WV: West Virginia University Libraries, Digital Publishing Institute, 2017. CC-BY.

[38] Dufour, Monique and Jennifer Ahern-Dodson. "Good Writers Always Follow My Rules." *Bad Ideas About Writing*. Edited by Cheryl E. Ball and Drew M. Loewe. Morgantown, WV: West Virginia University Libraries, Digital Publishing Institute, 2017. CC-BY.

[39] More about this in an upcoming chapter.

YES, THERE ARE NO RULES.

First,[40] if writing is simply a matter of following rules and plugging in formulas, it's boring to most people.

Second, in writing, problems are normal. When we think of writing as an opportunity to use and develop our repertoires to make and express meaning, writers can define the problems and needs before them and draw on their resources to solve them with creativity and aplomb. Perhaps we don't have as much uninterrupted time to write as we once did. We cannot create more time where there is none, but we can learn to write in the time we have. Perhaps our longer, more complex ideas cannot be crammed into a five-paragraph theme. We can learn new ways of organizing an essay to express an ambiguous claim. We don't need to stop writing when the rules don't work. And, we don't need to read and judge one another's writing only in terms of our own strictures. When we acknowledge that many of our rules are in fact techniques, and when we understand that writing is the skillful use of evolving repertoires, we can focus on expressing ideas worth sharing and become the kind of readers and writers who are in a position to listen.

QUESTIONS:

- When you read that statement, "problems are normal" when it comes to writing, what is your response?
- What do you think of the debunking of the Outline and Catch Hook rules?

[40] Snippet from = Dufour, Monique and Jennifer Ahern-Dodson. "Good Writers Always Follow My Rules." *Bad Ideas About Writing*. Edited by Cheryl E. Ball and Drew M. Loewe. Morgantown, WV: West Virginia University Libraries, Digital Publishing Institute, 2017. CC-BY.

YOU ARE ALSO A READER.

Saturday January 5, 2008[41]

I'm thinking about making a PPT based on this...

"You may not think of yourself as a reader and writer.
But you are doing both in the broadest sense all the time.
You're reading your world every day; you compose your life.
In the kitchen each A.M., you read the cupboards and refrigerator for breakfast options, cereal to eggs to bagels.
You read the weather and read your closet, choosing your clothes by a complicated writer's formula: what's clean, what represents who I want to be today, what's appropriate for the weather?
You read the newspaper, perhaps, choosing quickly which story engages you and which you don't need to read further.
You read everyone at school and at work.
You read the signs and ads and marquees on your way home and write your evening plan in your head: go to the mall, stop in to listen to the band at X, or stay home and watch Y on TV.
You steal your daily habits from your family (think about Thanksgiving meals), your friends (there are clothes you borrow, sayings you pick up), your developing age and tastes (as a child you never ate artichokes, but now...)
You steal the right office or school moves by watching others in the same or similar situations.
You see what I mean, I think."
–Wendy Bishop, "Reading, Stealing, and Writing Like a Writer," *Elements of Alternative Style*, 1997.
Posted 1/5/2008 at 4:20 PM

+

By the time[42] students arrive in college, stories beginning with "once upon a time" are long gone, and in their place are difficult and dense texts—often multimedia texts— from a range of fields each with its own set of conventions. Instead of drawing on models of early literacy education that focus on teaching reading and writing simultaneously, college and universities largely privilege writing over reading. This hierarchy is evidenced by the universal first-year writing requirement in American colleges and universities, as well as by writing across the curriculum programs. The integrated approach to teaching reading and writing falls away to students' peril and causes great frustration in the professors who often attribute students' struggles in their courses to poor writing ability, when these problems are often related to students'

---

[41] Blog entry by Sybil Priebe; licensed CC-BY.
[42] Snippet from = Carillo, Ellen C. "Reading and Writing Are Not Connected." *Bad Ideas About Writing*. Edited by Cheryl E. Ball and Drew M. Loewe. Morgantown, WV: West Virginia University Libraries, Digital Publishing Institute, 2017. CC-BY.

reading difficulties. While students' eyes may make their way over every word, that does not mean that students have comprehended a text or that they are prepared to successfully complete the writing tasks associated with the reading, which often involve summary, analysis, interpretation, and evaluation.

More importantly, if students are not given the opportunity to continue working on their reading throughout their college careers, they may struggle analyzing, interpreting, and evaluating all that surrounds them since comprehension is a crucial step toward these more advanced interpretive practices. Students may lack the ability to read the world around them because they do not have the tools to recognize the values and assumptions that inform the images, advertisements, news stories, political campaigns, and ideas with which they come into contact daily. By not focusing on reading as an equally creative and active enterprise as writing—very much writing's counterpart in the creation of meaning— colleges and universities are potentially producing students, or citizens, who think reading is passive. These students might blindly accept whatever comes their way rather than actively engaging ideas, asking questions, and seeking out multiple perspectives.

Although writing is more often thought of as a creative act, reading is just as creative. When one writes, one is creating meaning by putting words and ideas together. [...] This is why a few people might read the same novel[43] but each take something different from it. That personal transaction with the text has affected how each reader creates meaning. When reading and writing are taught alongside each other in the college-level classroom, students can gain practice experiencing and relishing in opportunities to create meaning not just through writing, but through reading everything from print texts to art to websites to national news events, all of which they will continue to engage beyond school. Focusing on active reading approaches, including everything from comprehension strategies to ways of determining something's inherent values and biases to productive methods of responding, is crucial if students are going to leave postsecondary institutions prepared to be informed, aware, and engaged citizens.

QUESTIONS:

- What did you like to read as a child? Why?
- What do you read now (social media counts!)? Why? What do you enjoy about reading what you do read?

ACTIVITY:

This chapter could be copied and pasted into an editable Google Doc so that students could annotate collaboratively and discuss their reading strategies.

---

[43] The original text does not place a comma here, but Microsoft Word wants to! It's understandable with or without the comma, isn't it?

READING STRATEGIES[44]

Most discussions and writing assignments–from brief responses to in-depth research papers–will depend on your ability to understand what you read. Following are some strategies for getting the most out of assigned readings.

- o **PURPOSE.** When you start a reading assignment, identify your purpose and write it down somewhere such as on a sticky that you put on the first page of the book or on your computer screen. Keep that information nearby and refer to it occasionally as you read.
- o **GOAL.** Your primary goal is to identify the main point, the idea the writer wants to communicate. Finding the main point helps you understand the details–the facts and explanations that develop and clarify the main point. It also helps you relate the reading to things you learned in class or in other assignments.
- o **PAUSE.** Regardless of what you read, stop occasionally and assess how well you understand what you are reading. If you aren't confident, go back and read it again. Don't just push ahead.[45]
- o **MARK IT UP.** The best way to remember the information you read is to do something physical with it, something beyond just letting your eyes scan the page. For example, taking notes as you read helps your brain retain the information.
- o **TALK ABOUT IT.** A good way to review and reinforce what you've learned is to discuss the reading with classmates. Discussions can help you determine whether your understanding is the same as that of your peers. They can also spark new ideas or insights.

+

Tuesday February 19, 2008

So, there were these two "experts" on *The Today Show* this morning... talking to [a host] about how Americans are "getting dumber." I had to chuckle to myself a few times. The woman was proclaiming that when students read online material, they don't connect it to the world around them like they would if they read books. Before I even jump into her claims, I had to wonder, "DO THESE TWO EXPERTS TEACH?" Are they trying to resolve this so-called problem? Now, as for the claims about reading, it seems like this woman has never read a blog. I mean, I use my blogs to CONSTANTLY connect to the world around me. And since I read others' blogs, I do the same. Connect to them. Whether I know them or not. AND, lastly, one CAN NOT force students to read read read. It loses all fun that way. One can only simply place a book in front of them that may spark some interest which will cause the domino effect; they'll want to read more. I read lots of Shakespeare when I was younger; what do I read now? Everything but "him" (yea, I'm one of "those people" who thinks he was probably a she or many, many people. Blasphemous, I know.) because I didn't connect to those plays AT ALL. Now, *Catcher in the Rye*,

---

[45] This tip might as well be called The Power of the Pause. Pause in your reading. Take a minute to understand that last sentence or paragraph.

yes! *Fahrenheit 451.* Yes. *To Kill a Mockingbird.* Yes. *1984. Animal Farm. Haroun the Sea of Stories. Why Men Love Bitches. You Just Don't Understand. Rule of the Bone.*

[…]

Are we getting "dumber"? It depends. On definitions... what does it mean to be "intelligent"? What does it mean to be "dumb"? It seemed like they were using the fact that, on average, we don't know who Bill Gates is (but we do recognize Harry Potter) or where Iraq is located to claim we are dumb. That's it? That's how we determine one from another? Based on just those items? Perhaps what they should've said was that those with "book smarts" are shrinking in population, but those with "street smarts" are not. What I worry about is the small thing they covered; it's "cool" to be "dumb."

Posted 2/19/2008 at 10:12 AM

QUESTIONS:

- Try to answer the questions in the last paragraph of the blog entry.
- Is it "cool" to be "appear stupid"?
- In what ways are you an "active reader"?
- Go back to the first blog post in this chapter – do you agree with Wendy Bishop about all the things you "read" each day?

THIRD BATCH OF EXERCISES

EXERCISE: RULES.

Make a list of all the rules you've been told about spelling and punctuation and grammar and reading and writing. Yes, we've been given a lot of rules, haven't we? Okay, so, before you rip the list up, look it over and think about where those rules come from. Are any of them helpful? Which ones did you learn easily, and which ones still trip you up? Conduct your own analysis of all this in a paragraph... What rules matter? What lessons are you taking away from the content in this chapter about writing and rules and subjectivity?

EXERCISE: READING TALLY.

Think of all the reading you do. Try to tally it all up – texting, email, to-do lists, homework. Estimate how many words you write weekly. Report that to your class/classmates. What are their estimates?

Now, ask yourself: How does taking in ALL those words affect who you are as a reader?

EXERCISE: DIY.

Create an exercise or activity that would assist students in reading more actively. Share that activity with your instructor. It might end up in this spot of the textbook!

HELPERS.

This chapter will cover the elements that should HELP students in learning, whether it's through writing or reading.

COLLEGE RESOURCES

If we try to handle every challenge alone, we can become frustrated and overwhelmed. Following are some resources available at NDSCS...[46]

- Your instructors can clarify information and give you strategies to succeed. To contact an instructor, use My Messages in Blackboard or email them directly using the email listed in their syllabus or by using the Directory on the NDSCS website.
- Tutors can help you see, understand, and fix problems before you submit work. You can find them over in Old Main (the building with the "S" on top).
- Tech support is available for Blackboard; you can find information on this by logging into Blackboard.
  - o If logging into Blackboard is the issue you are having, reach out to Distance Ed (use the Directory on the NDSCS website to find contact info).
- Librarians can quickly guide you to exactly the information you need. Contact information for the library is in the Directory on the NDSCS web site.
- Free, confidential counseling services can help a student cope with difficult personal situations or academic problems. Their information is available through the NDSCS Directory, too.
- Don't have a device or is yours not ultra-reliable? Seek out the computer labs on campus, bring a friend and/or some headphones, and conduct your own WORK ZONE.
- Advocate for yourself!

Many students are reluctant to seek help. They feel like doing so marks them as slow, weak, or demanding. The truth is, every learner occasionally struggles. If you are sincerely trying to keep up but feel over your head, ask for help as early as possible. Most instructors will work hard to help students who make the effort to help themselves.

REGARDING TECHNOLOGY:

- If you don't know how to use a computer or if you aren't all that confident in your computer skills, get some help. As you've noticed, we have class in a computer lab. You will need to know how to log on to our computers.
- Do you have a back-up if your computer gets a virus or your roommate decides to delete all of your work off of her computer? Consider saving all documents

---

[46] Edited from 1, 2, 3 Write! by Gay Monteverde is licensed under a Creative Commons Attribution-NonCommercial-ShareAlike 4.0 International License, except where otherwise noted.

you write for this course in a safe place like Google Drive and/or a flash drive. Strange things can happen when technology is involved. Be prepared.

- Even though we have all of this wonderful technology in front of us to use, please don't make that the focus of every class period. In other words, try to save your texting, email checking, and fantasy football roster trades for your free time.

QUESTIONS:

o Do you advocate for yourself? Give an example.

REFLECTION AND SELF-ASSESSMENT

This chunk covers the importance of reflecting on your learning and how to go about assessing your learning, too, if that process or activity is built into your course.

DEFINITION OF METACOGNITION

Metacognition is the process of thinking about thinking… Here are some questions we ask ourselves when we employ the process of metacognition, especially the third one called evaluating…

- Planning[47] - *What do I already know about this topic? How have I solved problems like this before? What should I do first?*
- Monitoring - *What should I look for in this reading or assignment? How should I proceed? What information is important to remember?*
- Evaluating - *What did I learn? Did I get the results I expected? What could I have done differently? Can I apply this way of thinking to other problems or situations? Is there anything I don't understand—any gaps in my knowledge? Do I need to go back through the task to fill in any gaps in understanding?*

CHANGE THE WAY YOU THINK.[48]

Reflection can be an invaluable tool in changing a person's thought patterns and responses to situations. Many people lapse into "auto-pilot," our day-to-day way of dealing with people, places, and situations. However, without frequent reflection and evaluation of the way we respond to these external stimuli, it can be easy to fall into patterns of behavior that are unproductive or even damaging. Reflection can help you actively assess your situation and reappraise it to feel more positive and in control.

ANALYZE EXPERIENCES.

You will have so many experiences every day that over the course of a lifetime it may be difficult to take stock of what they all meant. If you take the time to reflect each

---

47 Multiple Wikihow authors. "How to Put Metacognition in Process for Teachers." Wikihow. https://www.wikihow.com/Put-Metacognition-in-Process-for-Teachers Updated 07 Oct 21.

48 Rogers, Tracey. "How to Reflect." Wikihow. https://www.wikihow.com/Reflect Updated 26 March 20. Licensed Under an Attribution-Noncommercial-Share Alike 3.0 Creative Commons License

day on what a given experience meant right after it happened, however, it can be easier to process the event and your reaction to it.

Think about your reaction to the experience/assignment...
- How do you feel the experience/assignment went? Does that match how you anticipated the experience/assignment might go? Why or why not?
- Did you learn anything from the experience/assignment? Is there anything you can take away from the experience/assignment that will help you better understand yourself, other people, or the world around you?
- Does the experience/assignment you had affect the way you think or feel? Why, and in what way?
- What can you learn about yourself from the experience/assignment and the way you reacted to it?

DON'T CRITICIZE OR BEAT YOURSELF UP AS YOU REFLECT.[49]

Self-reflection isn't about judging or criticizing your past decisions. Instead, self-reflection helps you learn from your past so you can reach a healthier, happier future.
- Instead of thinking "I can't believe I made that mistake," think "I'm glad I have the opportunity to reflect on my mistakes so I can do better in the future."
- Instead of thinking, "I shouldn't have X," think "I'm now better prepared for X."

QUESTIONS:

- Let's return to the "Analyzing Experiences" part of this chunk of information. Think back on ANY assignment or project you've completed in ANY class and answer at least half of these questions:
  - *How do you feel the experience/assignment went? Does that match how you anticipated the experience/assignment might go? Why or why not?*
  - *Did you learn anything from the experience/assignment? Is there anything you can take away from the experience/assignment that will help you better understand yourself, other people, or the world around you?*
  - *Does the experience/assignment you had affect the way you think or feel? Why, and in what way?*
  - *What can you learn about yourself from the experience/assignment and the way you reacted to it?*
- Let's return to the "evaluating" part of metacognition. Ask yourself these questions about a current project:
  - *What did I learn?*
  - *Did I get the results I expected?*
  - *What could I have done differently?*
  - *Can I apply this way of thinking to other problems or situations? Is there anything I don't understand—any gaps in my knowledge?*
  - *Do I need to go back through the task to fill in any gaps in understanding?*

---

[49] Klaphaak, Adrian and Janice Tieperman. "How to Self-Reflect." *Wikihow.* https://www.wikihow.com/Self-Reflect Updated 29 Oct 21. Licensed Under an Attribution-Noncommercial-Share Alike 3.0 Creative Commons License.

PEER WORKSHOPS AND FEEDBACK

Peer workshops and receiving feedback are typically a HUGE part of most writing/composition courses. It might be difficult for some students to receive feedback from others but always remember: writing is subjective. Since it is, the best other humans can do is give you their opinions based on the things they've read (remember: everyone is a writer and everyone is a reader). With that said, this chunk of information breaks down peer workshops (or peer review sessions) into manageable pieces... THREE pieces, to be exact.

Peer revision[50] has added benefits over self-revision. Other people can notice things in your paper that you didn't. Other humans might ask questions or give you suggestions you HAD NOT considered, which may be uber helpful.

Some instructors set aside class time for peer review, but even if your instructor doesn't, it's a good idea to seek out feedback from a classmate, roommate, a tutor (if your college has a tutoring center), or anyone who can offer a fresh perspective.

POSSIBLE STEPS IN THE PEER REVIEW PROCESS:

1. Exchange a draft with a classmate, or group of classmates. This might be done online.
2. Read it. (You might want to read it aloud?)
3. Give feedback based on the table below.
4. Revise your own draft taking into account the feedback you receive.

FEEDBACK STRATEGY: WWW / TAG

WWW	TAG	Examples
WOW.	T – Tell classmate something that WOW'd you about their draft.	Your introduction is very controversial; this will shock readers.
What If...	A – Ask a question about the content in the draft.	Why did you leave out the history of how you met this weird person?
I Wonder...	G – Give a suggestion to your classmate about their draft.	I would add in more details about the situation that lead you to deciding that adoption was the route you were going to take.

QUESTIONS:

- Are you open to the kinds of feedback you'll get using that table above with the WWW/TAG pieces?
- What do you typically want feedback on when it comes to projects and papers? Why?
- What do you feel comfortable giving feedback to classmates on? Why?

---

[50] "Basic Writing/Print version." *Wikibooks, The Free Textbook Project*. 9 Sep 2008, 16:02 UTC. 11 May 2016, 17:37 <https://en.wikibooks.org/w/index.php?title=BasicWriting/Printversion&oldid=1273791>. Licensed CC-BY-SA.

UNGRADING

If writing is subjective then assessing writing is subjective.
Boom!

+

Indeed,[51] grading does very little. Music theory teacher Kris Shaffer says that "letter grades do an absolutely horrible job" of three things that would help students improve their writing: (1) determining whether students understand a concept well enough to implement it, (2) identifying elements of student writing that need improvement, and (3) helping students learn to better self-assess. Shaffer makes his argument specifically about writing music, but I've recast it here for writing words. Each of these three goals presents a helpful perspective on developing authors' needs. An author's ability to compose requires skill, understanding, and situational familiarity. None of those goals are met through a letter grade. Grades help label, sort, and rank students; they don't inform students, target instruction, or encourage self-awareness. Those who have left school and begun their careers have long stopped expecting grades to help determine what they do and don't do well because grades aren't appropriate measures of learning. Schools need to stop relying on grades, too.

Instead, we should teach people how to improve their writing through reflection and peer review. Variations of peer review help us write in many of our day-to-day situations. We learn what sorts of text messages work best by observing how our friends text and respond to us. We learn what makes an effective email by reading the ones we get and responding or deleting as we see fit. We learn how best to craft Facebook posts by seeing what kinds of content can garner the most likes—at its heart a form of quick (and addictive) peer review. Consider, too, all of the review features available on websites such as Yelp, Amazon, LinkedIn, Angie's List, and so on. Reviews offer feedback and critique by users/peers.

In other words, situations, not teachers, define the importance of writing.

If grades tell nothing meaningful about writing ability, and if learning to work as/with peer reviewers provides insights into and feedback about writing performance, then the traditional structure of writing education is backward.

Writing should not be done for a grade. Teachers should not grade writing; instead, they should empower their students to meaningfully assess the effectiveness of writing.

QUESTIONS:

- o Do you learn more when you have intrinsic reasons versus extrinsic ones? Give an example…
- o What does it mean to you to know you may assess yourself and your learning in this course?
- o When have you written effectively for a situation, and not a teacher?

---

[51] Snippet from = Friend, Christopher R. "Student Writing Must Be Graded By The Teacher." *Bad Ideas About Writing*. Edited by Cheryl E. Ball and Drew M. Loewe. Morgantown, WV: West Virginia University Libraries, Digital Publishing Institute, 2017. CC-BY.

WᴬTSKY ✓
@gwatsky

always work on two projects at once. that way you can procrastinate on project A by messing around on project B, and when you get tired of project B you can waste time by working on project A. you will be twice as productive while doing nothing but procrastinate

PROCRASTINATION[52]

Is procrastination always bad? Or is it a necessary part of your writing process? What is it? What does it look like for you? For some people, having a writing assignment suddenly stirs a desire to clean, go for a walk, catch up on chores—do anything other than write. That's procrastination. Vacuuming CAN be the same as taking time to think about your topic or assignment unless you never get to the actual writing.

HOW TO USE PROCRASTINATION

If you know that you have a tendency to procrastinate, you can analyze your habits to find a way to get back to productive work. If you just have difficulty getting the words onto the page, you might try some techniques that don't feel like writing but produce results. Try some of these:

- **Bribe friends to listen and/or scribe.** If you have more trouble with getting the words on the page, but like to talk over your ideas, invite a friend out for coffee or lunch in exchange for helping you out by writing down what you say about your assignment.
- **Use dictation software.** Dictation software allows you to speak your ideas while the software captures your words onto the page. You may have dictation software already available on your own computer (Google Docs and Microsoft Word call it Voice to Text); it may be provided by your school; or you may find a free mobile application.
- **Use downtime to freewrite.** If your problem is that you don't have enough big chunks of time, use the time you do have for some freewriting. That means keeping a notebook or electronic device (or a Notes app) handy so that you can fit in a quick bit of writing while you are riding the bus, stuck waiting at an appointment, or in between classes.
- **Set a limit to procrastination.** Limiting procrastination may be necessary if you find that you just waste time, or you may need to ask someone else for help. If you find yourself procrastinating with social media or some other distraction, set a time limit on that activity and use an alarm.
- **Set aside writing time**. If you find time to do everything but work on your assignment, then you may need to set appointments with yourself to ensure that you have enough time set aside to write your paper.
- **Get an accountability partner.** Some people find that they accomplish more by working with another person or a group that they feel accountable to. Having a regular meeting or a scheduled check-in where you have to show your work can ensure that you get it done.

---

[52] *The Word on College Reading and Writing* by Carol Burnell, Jaime Wood, Monique Babin, Susan Pesznecker, and Nicole Rosevear is licensed under a Creative Commons Attribution-NonCommercial 4.0 International License, except where otherwise noted.

ASKING FOR AND GETTING HELP[53]

- If you are having trouble getting started on a project, try reading the samples offered by your instructor – or in this book. They might jump start ideas for your own paper/project.
- When researching, head to your local library (if your college doesn't have one). Ask the librarian to help you, if you feel comfortable enough; they might appreciate a break from their duties to help out, and they are knowledgeable of their space.
- If you aren't a native English speaker, and you want your paper to "sound like it came from a white person," you might want to consider buying a grammar handbook.
  - o Honestly, adding in your first language (or dialects) *should* be cool with most teachers; it adds to your voice and authenticity.
  - o And, by the way, we're aware that the English language is a goofy language... just the slang alone is hard to keep up with!

QUESTIONS:

- o How comfortable do you feel asking for help, from teachers or tutors or librarians?
- o <insert more questions created by students>

---

[53] "Writing Better University Essays/Common essay problems." *Wikibooks, The Free Textbook Project*. 9 Apr 2015, 08:11 UTC. 11 May 2016, 16:20 <https://en.wikibooks.org/w/index.php?title=WritingBetterUniversityEssays/Commonessayproblems&oldid=2840084>. Licensed CC-BY-SA.

LAST BATCH OF EXERCISES

EXERCISE: FEEDBACK

Find a classmate's writing to give feedback to and practice the WWW/TAG approach.

EXERCISE: RANDOM STARTER QUESTIONS

- What would you be doing if you were not going to college?
- If you could start a charity, what would your cause be?
- If you ran the world, what rules or laws would you put into place and why?

EXERCISE: YOUR NAME

Look up what your name means, if you don't know already. In a few paragraphs, explain how your name describes who you are (or does not).

Then, create a poem using each letter of your first name (in order) as the first letter of line. Use that line to describe who you are to your class/classmates/teacher.

Example of Name Poem:
S – Sarcastic
Y – Young-at-heart
B – Blasphemous
I – Intuitive
L – Listener

EXERCISE: EXPERT

Everyone is great at something - write about what you do best. It could be a hobby, a sport, reading, playing chess, or anything else you excel at.

ACTIVITY: DISCUSSION ABOUT GOALS[54]

Take two or three minutes to list as many of your own current goals that you can think of. These might be academic goals, professional goals, or personal goals. For instance, you might want to learn more about a certain academic subject or achieve a degree or certification. You might want to advance yourself in your current career, or you might want to find a job in a completely new field than the one you're working in right now. You might want to gain a new skill that will help you with a hobby that you enjoy.

Now, consider how writing might be a useful tool in helping you to achieve some of these goals. Can writing help you to explore, to create, to understand, to persuade, or to share in ways that can help you reach some of these goals? You might be asked to discuss your thoughts with some classmates in a small group, and if class time allows for it, your small group might share some conclusions about the value of writing with the whole class.

ACTIVITY: JOURNAL OR BLOG[55]

Consider the value of keeping a journal or a blog. How can you use this form to help in your other writing? To reflect on experiences? To sharpen your observational skill and engage your world on a daily basis?

Today there are a lot of options for journaling, and it can be private or very public. Many people choose to keep blogs that cover adventures, traveling, daily life, and relationships. They may chronicle small adventures on social media like Twitter, Facebook, Instagram or Tumblr. Sites like Blogger and Wordpress have provided a direct forum for those who want to go public with their most private thoughts.

ACTIVITY: PERSONAL VS ACADEMIC[56]

What is "personal writing"? What is "academic writing"?

For this activity, write about the terms "personal writing" and "academic writing" and what they mean to you.

The goal of a freewrite is to keep your pen or pencil to the paper (or fingers typing) for the entire length of time. It is natural for the mind to wander. Often in life we are thinking of many things at the same time: class, how hungry we are, what time it is. When you feel as if you have run out of things to say or you find you can no longer focus on the topic, don't stop writing! Simply continue to write about what is distracting you and carefully make your way back to the topic.

These pieces are not collected or graded, so do not edit yourself. Write whatever comes to mind in response to the prompt. We will try to define the two terms as a group based on everyone's contributions.

[54] *The Word on College Reading and Writing* by Carol Burnell, Jaime Wood, Monique Babin, Susan Pesznecker, and Nicole Rosevear is licensed under a Creative Commons Attribution-NonCommercial 4.0 International License, except where otherwise noted.
[55] *Teaching Autoethnography: Personal Writing in the Classroom* by Melissa Tombro is licensed under a Creative Commons Attribution-NonCommercial-ShareAlike 4.0 International License, except where otherwise noted.
[56] *Teaching Autoethnography: Personal Writing in the Classroom* by Melissa Tombro is licensed under a Creative Commons Attribution-NonCommercial-ShareAlike 4.0 International License, except where otherwise noted.

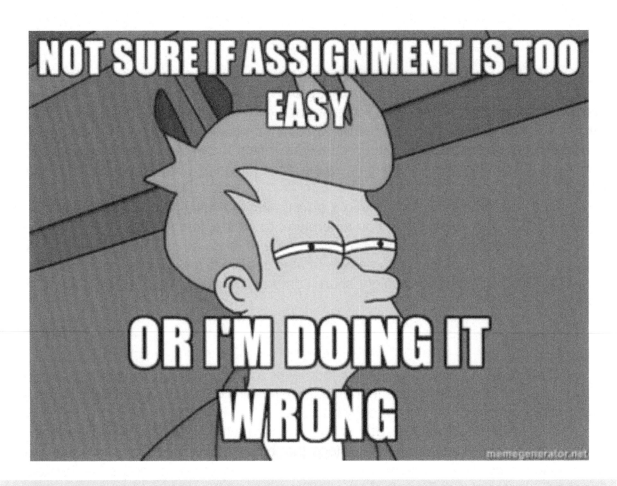

CHAPTER 2: THE WRITING PROCESS

Take the following nuggets – or "strict" steps in the writing process – with a grain of salt. Follow them or don't follow them; it's up to you.

WRITING IS THINKING ON PAPER.

WRITING IS THE TANGIBLE RESULT OF THINKING.[57]

Please note: The writing process is something that no two people will do the same way. There is no "right way" or "wrong way" to write. It can be a very messy and fluid process, and the following is only a representation of commonly used steps. Just in case you weren't aware of this already:

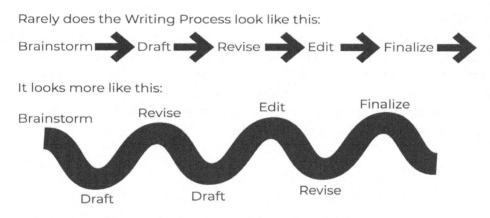

Rarely does the Writing Process look like this:

Brainstorm ➡ Draft ➡ Revise ➡ Edit ➡ Finalize ➡

It looks more like this:

Brainstorm — Revise — Edit — Finalize
Draft — Draft — Revise

This visual was created by Sybil Priebe using Piktochart.com.

Now, some say learning how to think—how to develop your own ideas and concepts—is the purpose of a college education. Even though the end result of writing is typically a product of some sort, writing itself is a process through which you ask questions; create, develop, hone, and organize ideas; argue a point; search for evidence to support your ideas…and so on. The point here is that writing really involves creative and critical thinking processes. Like any creative process, it often starts in a jumble as you develop, sort, and sift through ideas. But it doesn't need to stay in disarray. Your writing will gain direction as you start examining those ideas. It just doesn't happen all at once. Writing is a process that happens over time.

---

[57] From the Excelsior Online Writing Lab (OWL), 2019. This site is licensed under a CC-BY license. https://owl.excelsior.edu/writing-process/writing-process-overview/

BRAINSTORMING & PREWRITING.

QUESTIONS:

- Do you think you need to brainstorm or outline before creating certain projects? Why or why not?
- Why do people (teachers and writers) value brainstorming and prewriting, in your opinion?

WHY PREWRITE?[58]

Prewriting for even 5 to 20 minutes can help you establish what you already know about a paper topic, as well as aid you in discovering where you would like to go with a paper (i.e. what you want to know). It can reveal to you those potential areas of personal interest within the writing task: in a manner of speaking, prewriting enables you to "discover" yourself within the context of your topic. Also, prewriting can act as a tool to ward off or break through what is commonly called "writer's block" since you're throwing down EVERYTHING in your head about topic right now!

BRAINSTORMING & PREWRITING:

Brainstorming is one of the most effective pre-writing techniques you can use. It's virtually painless and can be pretty fun, if you let it be! Let your mind wander and think about things that you would like to explore more. Try to create a mental web of things you can connect to one another. Let the lightning of ideas strike you as they may. If you'd like a bit more structure in your prewriting, try one of these methods: Listing, Freewriting, Outling, and Clustering. Here are examples of those methods:

LISTING:

IF the assignment is an essay about anything you want to learn more about, perhaps you might wonder how other humans in college find BALANCE.

1. Balancing classes and work
2. Studying better and more efficiently
3. Distant friendships vs finding new ones on campus
4. How do I find time to take care of myself?

FREEWRITING:

IF the assignment is to identify one's teaching philosophy:

---

[58] "Basic Writing/Print version." *Wikibooks, The Free Textbook Project.* 9 Sep 2008, 16:02 UTC. 11 May 2016, 18:08 <https://en.wikibooks.org/w/index.php?title=BasicWriting/Printversion&oldid=1273791>. Licensed CC-BY-SA.

Thursday January 23, 2003[59]

In one of my own classes, I have to come up with my Teaching Philosophy.. theories as to how and why I teach, etc.. also theories/analyzations behind the assignments I assign. Hmm.. here's a freewrite about those things:

First off, Teaching for me is like a religion.. it is my religion. I come to the school to 'worship' if you will. My purpose in life is to teach.. it is my calling, I guess. Expressivism comes through this because I want students to express themselves in my classroom. I want them to be the 'best' they can be.. the best writer, the best student. And I want to TRY to inspire that. TRY= Key word. I figure that by getting them to look at themselves, they will grow and better what they have and thus, the community of people surrounding them will get better too. The Social Epistemics have good ideas that I latch onto as far as having the students question everything around them... but I don't want them to worry so much about controlling or analyzing those items/people around them. They should, in my opinion, start with something they do know the answers to, something familiar- themselves and the way they work. Work from the inside out, I suppose. Again, in connecting to religions, I think of Buddhism which in contrast to, say, Catholicism wants it's followers to be the best 'them' whereas Catholicism wants us to imitate Jesus. WWJD. Well, I ask- who cares what he'd do- what are YOU going to do? What is the best for YOU? Perhaps that's also why I shy away from having students read a lot of what others have written because while I don't mind if they want to mimic another writer, I do want them to write the way THEY feel it should come out. I mean, sure, I wanted at one time to write poetry like e.e. cummings, but then I thought- wait, I am the only Sybil Ann Priebe that is ever going to live... maybe I should perfect MY VOICE and MY STYLE and not try to be someone else. There are lessons that can be learned from reading others, definitely, I just don't think that I want students to feel that their voice or style (weird or traditional as it is) isn't important- ESPECIALLY after they have been working through paper after paper at growing in their writing skills.

Assignments: I want my assignments to be just like my classroom atmosphere: fun, open/flexible, and interesting (adding in the intellectual side- LEARNING SOMETHING).
Posted 1/23/2003 at 12:38 PM

OUTLINE:

IF the assignment is an argument about WHY balance is necessary, here's a possible outline that could be followed:
- A. Intro: Why We Need Balance
  - i. Mental/Spiritual
  - ii. Academic
  - iii. Financial
- B. Obstacles to Finding Balance
  - i. People

55

ii.   Stress and Illness
C. Who Has Found Balance?
    i.   Examples
D. Tips on Finding Balance
    i.   Be Organized
    ii. Find Routines that work for you

CLUSTERING:

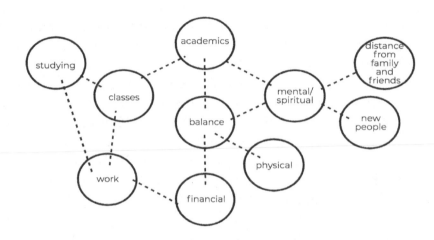

EXERCISE: OPENING SENTENCES

Choose one of the following topics, and practice[60] writing a few opening sentences. Then, maybe, share with others in class or online. Look at their opening sentences. How would you rewrite their sentences, if at all? Why? Discuss your changes and listen to how your peers have revised your sentences. Taking in other people's ideas will help you see new ways to approach your own writing and thinking.

Topics:
- Facing fears
- Safety in sports
- Community policing
- Educating prisoners
- Sex education
- A book or movie that impacted you
- One thing you would change about your community
- Beauty standards
- Toxic masculinity
- How the media affects identity formation
- Gender roles
- Race in America
- The value of art in society
- Travel as part of a well-rounded education
- Drugs and alcohol
- Advice to new parents
- Advice to teachers
- The value of making mistakes
- How you'd spend a million dollars
- What a tough day at work taught you about yourself or others.

[60] *The Word on College Reading and Writing* by Carol Burnell, Jaime Wood, Monique Babin, Susan Pesznecker, and Nicole Rosevear is licensed under a Creative Commons Attribution-NonCommercial 4.0 International License, except where otherwise noted.

DRAFTING.

THE CRUMMY ROUGH DRAFT

A rough draft[61] is an important step in the writing process. Writing more than one draft gives you the opportunity to catch problems and see where the paper may not be working. You may want to do an outline to plan your paper beforehand but doing that is not always necessary. After you choose your topic, any possible research and or sources needed in order you can begin actually writing. While you write your rough draft, you may not feel completely satisfied about the paper, but that's okay because that is what a rough draft is for. You want to give yourself a chance to work to get to the best arrangement of ideas and find different ways of expressing them.

The Importance of Just Getting It on The Page:
Not much can be done for a piece of writing until it is on paper or computer screen. You may worry that the paper will not be very good or even think that it will be awful, yet you won't really know until you've actually written it. Not only will you and your reader(s) not be able to see what you have written, but there is no chance of working to fix what has not yet been written.

WRITE "BADLY"

You might want to believe in the importance of writing "badly."[62] Bruce Ballenger, writer and professor of English at Boise State[63] explains why writing badly is an important part of the writing process:

Giving myself permission to write badly makes it much more likely that I will write what I don't expect to write, and from those surprises will come some of my best writing. Writing badly is also a convenient alternative to staring off into space and waiting for inspiration.

Sometimes the biggest problem writers have with getting started is that they feel like the writing needs to be good, or well organized, or they feel like they need to start at the beginning. None of that is true. All you need to do is start.

Have you ever seen a potter make a clay pot? Before a potter can start shaping or throwing a pot, they have to bring the big wet blob of clay and slap it down on the table. It's heavy and wet and messy, but it's the essential raw material. No clay? No pot. Starting to write anything is a lot like that. You have to dump all the words and ideas onto the table. Just get them out. Only then do you have the raw material you

---

[61] "Basic Writing/Print version." *Wikibooks, The Free Textbook Project.* 9 Sep 2008, 16:02 UTC. 11 May 2016, 18:08 <https://en.wikibooks.org/w/index.php?title=BasicWriting/Printversion&oldid=1273791>. Licensed CC-BY-SA.
[62] And yes, "writing badly" is as subjective as "writing well." But that means your "bad writing" isn't probably all that "bad," you know. It's probably just fine! Isn't that a nice thought?
[63] There should be a comma here, right? Why didn't they put one? Because punctuation – just like grammar and writing and all that jazz – is SUBJECTIVE!

need to start shaping the words into something beautiful and lasting. You can wait until the revision stages to worry about shaping your writing to be its "best." For now, just get the ideas on the table.

EMBRACE REALITY

Don't imagine the situation of your writing assignment to be any better or worse than it really is.[64] There are some important truths for you to recognize:

- Focus on what you do best rather than fretting about your perceived weaknesses.
- Acknowledge that writing can be difficult and that all you need to do is do your best.
- Recognize what might be new or unfamiliar about the type of writing that you're doing.
- Understand that confusion and frustration is a natural part of experiencing new things, and it's okay; it's part of the learning process.
- Remember that you're a student and that you're supposed to be experiencing things that are new and unfamiliar (new formats, new audiences, new subject matter, new processes, new approaches, etc.).
- Repeat the mantra: "It doesn't have to be perfect; it just has to be DONE."

QUESTIONS:

- o What does it mean to "write badly" to you?
- o Is the clay pot analogy too cheesy?
- o What do you think when you hear "it doesn't have to be perfect; it just has to be done"?

---

[64] *The Word on College Reading and Writing* by Carol Burnell, Jaime Wood, Monique Babin, Susan Pesznecker, and Nicole Rosevear is licensed under a Creative Commons Attribution-NonCommercial 4.0 International License, except where otherwise noted.

REVISING.

Some say your first draft[65] shouldn't be your final draft. Some say that no draft is ever perfect, but sometimes, a writer can hit the nail on the head the first time. So, think of revision in this manner: You have to have content to work with before you revise. After you have completed drafting your ideas and have established what you consider to be a complete product of the thoughts you intend to convey, then dive into the revision process. Revising is more than correcting spelling errors; it's finding clarity of thought. It could even be finding new thoughts you didn't have before you started the paper. You might find yourself getting rid of extra fluff.

STEPS

1. **Read carefully** over your draft several times, with a different purpose in mind to check a specific problem each time. Look first for content (what you said), then organization (your arrangement of ideas), and finally style (the way you use words).
2. **Listen carefully.** Read your paper aloud for confusing statements or awkward wording. Try reading it backward, even. This might seem REALLY nerdy, but it will help you! Listen for the paper's flow and pay attention to details one idea to the next. Each idea should come to some sort of conclusion while introducing the next idea, and each idea should relate to the one before it and the one after it.
3. **Take time** between readings. Allow yourself time to finish a paper so you can put it aside and read it fresh when you go back to it later, to be more objective.
4. **Ask yourself these questions:**
   a. Are you saying what you mean to say?
   b. Will your audience understand it?
   c. Does it accomplish the purpose of the project or paper or activity/assignment?

QUESTIONS:

- How do you revise your work? What's your process?
- After drafting and revising for a project, ask yourself the questions in #4 above.

---

[65] "Basic Writing/Print version." *Wikibooks, The Free Textbook Project*. 9 Sep 2008, 16:02 UTC. 11 May 2016, 17:39 <https://en.wikibooks.org/w/index.php?title=BasicWriting/Printversion&oldid=1273791>. Licensed CC-BY-SA.

EDITING.

WHAT IS EDITING?[66]

After you feel you've revised the draft as much as is needed, editing comes into play. Editing involves a number of small changes in a draft that can make a big difference in the draft's readability and coherence. Editing can happen at several points in the drafting and revision processes – not just at the end to "fix" things that are wrong.

So, what kinds of things happen when editing? Here are a few:
- word changes
- minor sentence rearrangement
- added transitions
- changes for clarity
- minor deletions

WHAT SHOULD I EDIT FOR?

The main areas that should be addressed in editing are: Content and Structure. When editing the **content** of your writing, it is important to make sure your work has a clear focus or main idea. By asking yourself a few questions, you can avoid incomplete thoughts and/or irrelevant material. The following is a checklist you can use in editing your content:
- I have discovered what is important about my topic.
- I have expressed the main idea clearly.
- I have removed material that is unnecessary, confusing, or irrelevant.

Editing for **structure** ensures that your ideas are presented in a logical[67] order. A single idea[68] should be represented in each paragraph. Transitions serve to make the relationships between ideas clear. The following checklist is helpful in editing structure:
- My ideas are logically connected to one another.
- Each paragraph deals with only one major idea.
- I have included appropriate transitional words or phrases.

QUESTIONS:
- What kinds of things do you need help editing the most when it comes to your own projects and papers?

---

[66] "Basic Writing/Print version." *Wikibooks, The Free Textbook Project.* 9 Sep 2008, 16:02 UTC. 11 May 2016, 17:39 <https://en.wikibooks.org/w/index.php?title=BasicWriting/Printversion&oldid=1273791>. Licensed CC-BY-SA.
[67] Please note that sometimes one's "logical order" might not look the same to everyone.
[68] But let's be real: sometimes, there is more than one idea in each paragraph!

PROOFREADING.

Proofreading[69] is the process of carefully reviewing a text for errors, especially surface errors such as spelling, punctuation, grammar, formatting, and typing errors. So, refining the **mechanics** in the proofreading phase prevents the reader from being distracted from your ideas. Here's a checklist can also help you catch these errors in your writing:

- I have used punctuation marks and capitalization correctly.
- I have checked the spelling of unfamiliar words.
- All subjects and verbs agree, if necessary to the flow and meaning of the content.
- I have corrected run-ons and sentence fragments, if they are confusing.
- I have used words with the correct meanings in their proper context.

WHEN SHOULD I EDIT OR PROOFREAD?

A major question that students will probably find themselves asking is this: How do I know when to edit a paper? How do I know it's time to proofread? As a matter of fact, there is no simple answer to those questions. Writing is a process that involves several steps, and these steps do not always occur in a straight line. Writing any sort of text is a circular rather than a linear process. Writers are rarely completely finished with one step, even after they move onto the next.

Most people tend to think that editing tends to happen sometime near the completion of the paper. In fact, that is not always the case. While the most important part of writing is simply the ability to express yourself and get ideas across, it can sometimes be helpful to take a quick break from drafting or revising and to spend some time editing (or even proofread a bit). Sometimes, playing with word choice, sentence structure, or transitions can help stimulate your mind, leading to new ideas. Thus, it's important to realize that editing is not necessarily a one-step action, but rather something that can be done throughout the entire writing process.

QUESTIONS:

- <insert questions here created by students>

---

[69] "Basic Writing/Print version." *Wikibooks, The Free Textbook Project.* 9 Sep 2008, 16:02 UTC. 11 May 2016, 17:39 <https://en.wikibooks.org/w/index.php?title=BasicWriting/Printversion&oldid=1273791>. Licensed CC-BY-SA.

Ivy
@Ivyzenati

I changed the sound of my alarm clock to hand clapping sounds 👏 to get all the recognition I deserve when I wake up at 7AM.

CHAPTER 3: PRACTICE

WHAT'S THE SITUATION?

There is no such thing as writing in general.[70] Do you doubt this claim? Test it out. Attempt to write something in general. Do not write for any specific audience, purpose, or context. Do not use any conventions that you've learned for school, work, creative writing, and so on. Just write in general.

You can't do it, because it can't be done. There is no such thing as writing in general. Writing is always in particular.

It's not just common sense that tells us that learning to write in general is not possible. Many studies of writing have been done— in workplaces, in classes across the college landscape, and in social and civic settings. They tell us that every new situation, audience, and purpose requires writers to learn to do and understand new possibilities and constraints for their writing. Writing fan fiction requires understanding what other fans expect, what fan fiction writers and readers think good fan fiction is, and what the technological medium supports and allows. The same is true for any other kind of writing—we write in our journals and think of our future selves or anyone who might find the journal. We write as biologists for other specialists who understand previous findings and value the ideas of some biologists more than others. As students write across their general education courses, they find themselves repeatedly asked to write essays or research papers, but often learn the hard way that their history teacher, poetry teacher, and philosophy teacher all mean and expect very different things by "essay" or "research paper." This is because context, audience, purpose, medium,

[70] Snippet from = Wardle, Elizabeth. "You Can Learn to Write in General." *Bad Ideas About Writing*. Edited by Cheryl E. Ball and Drew M. Loewe. Morgantown, WV: West Virginia University Libraries, Digital Publishing Institute, 2017. CC-BY.

history, and values of the community all impact what writing is and needs to be in each situation.

A better conception of writing is one in which we all remember (realistically) our own experiences learning to write in different situations, and then apply that memory to our expectations of what we and others are capable of achieving. A better notion of how writing works is one that recognizes that after learning scribal skills (letters, basic grammatical constructions), everything a writer does is impacted by the situation in which they are writing. And thus, they are going to have to learn again in each new situation. Yes, they can apply and repurpose some of what they already know how to do, but they will have to learn new things and not expect that what they already know about writing is easily applicable in new situations.

These ideas—that there is no writing in general, that writers always have more to learn, that failing or struggling are a normal part of writing—are some of the many threshold concepts of the discipline of writing studies. In other words, they are things researchers have learned, and things that will help writers be more effective, if only they can accept them in place of the common cultural assumptions about writing that are not always accurate.

QUESTIONS:

1. Do you agree that it's practically impossible to write "in general"?
2. What are some things you've written/created for SPECIFIC purposes or situations or audiences?

CHAPTER 3.1: THE RHETORICAL SITUATION.

"THE WHAT?"[71]

This is a typical response from students when first introduced to the concept of the rhetorical situation. The thing is, most of us intuitively understand rhetorical situations we face every day, but we give them little thought.

Consider this. You [the author] need to ask your parents [the audience] for money [the purpose]. It's the third time this semester you've asked, and it's right before the holidays [the context]. Should you communicate with a text, phone call, email, or Facebook message, and should it be funny, serious, or heartfelt [text]?

This is a rhetorical situation.

The rhetorical situation consists of:
- **Author:** The writer of the communication
- **Audience:** The receiver of the communication
- **Purpose:** The goal of the communication
- **Context:** The surrounding setting, time, culture, and social discussions on the topic
- **Text:** The genre, organization, and style of the communication
  - Genre is the form or shape.[72]
  - Writing strategies such as narration, description, or compare/contrast help develop and organize the content.[73]
  - Style is created through elements such as tone, diction, and syntax.[74]

The Rhetorical Situation asks students to consider all of the above when they begin to write something.

Returning to the scenario, you decide that the best way to convince your parents to send you money is through an honest email that explains why you are short on money. You choose this genre because you know that your parents will read it at home after work and prefer email to texts. You also thoughtfully write in a style that doesn't sound demanding but provide clear reasons why you need the money. How could they say no to that?

That's the power of understanding and analyzing what shapes the rhetorical situation. It helps you create audience-centered communication in the genre and style best suited to achieve your purpose.

+

---

[71] Anderson, Dana. "Rhetorical Situation." *Writing Unleashed*, Version 1. NDSCS; 2016.
[72] More information on Genres in the Genres Chapter.
[73] More information on Strategies in the Strategies Chapter.
[74] There may be more information on these items in the Nerd Chapter.

PURPOSE[75]

Often, you'll know your purpose at the exact moment you know your audience because they're generally a package deal:

- I need to write a letter to my landlord explaining why my rent is late so she won't be upset. (Audience = landlord; Purpose = explaining/keeping her happy)
- I want to write a proposal for my work team to persuade them to change our schedule. (Audience = work team; Purpose = persuading/to get the schedule changed)
- I have to write a research paper for my environmental science instructor comparing solar to wind power. (Audience = instructor; Purpose = analyzing/showing that you understand these two power sources)

QUESTIONS:

- Ask yourself, when given a project, these questions:
  - What is the assignment's purpose?
  - What is its audience?
  - What is the context of this project?
  - What will the end product/text/genre look like?

[75] *The Word on College Reading and Writing* by Carol Burnell, Jaime Wood, Monique Babin, Susan Pesznecker, and Nicole Rosevear is licensed under a Creative Commons Attribution-NonCommercial 4.0 International License, except where otherwise noted.

CHAPTER 3.2: EXPERIMENTATION.

Rule-driven writing instruction[76] may intend to make writing easier, but it often undermines the very skills it is designed to foster.

We propose another way. Think of good writing as the thoughtful use of an evolving repertoire, rather than adherence to a static list of commandments. In order to become a skillful writer, one discovers and experiments with a range of techniques. A writer draws upon this repertoire to meet the needs of the project, the ideas at hand, and the rhetorical situation. As one's repertoire grows, and as one becomes practiced in drawing upon it, one can grow more confident about overcoming difficulties, taking up challenges, and expressing one's ideas effectively. Ultimately, writers become skillful when they are willing to assess and reassess the quality of any idea about writing in terms of its effectiveness in their own experiences.

+

No one[77] knows what students will be asked to write five years from now, what not-yet-invented writing projects they'll face. They need these analytical skills to tackle writing needs in their future professions.

If young people are to be knowledgeable, ever-learning, active citizens in a participatory democracy, they must develop a wide-ranging, flexible literacy. Writing instructors should help students become informed, alert, and engaged readers and writers of a variety of texts and contexts, so that they learn to notice, appreciate, and master (should they so desire) all kinds of writing.

QUESTIONS:

1. What techniques or genres do you already know to write (with/within)?
2. What techniques or genres do you want to know more about?
3. What challenges do you see in practicing various genres?
4. What kind of writing would potentially spark JOY in you?

---

[76] Snippet from = Dufour, Monique and Jennifer Ahern-Dodson. "Good Writers Always Follow My Rules." *Bad Ideas About Writing*. Edited by Cheryl E. Ball and Drew M. Loewe. Morgantown, WV: West Virginia University Libraries, Digital Publishing Institute, 2017. CC-BY.
[77] Snippet from = Dunn, Patricia A. "Teaching Grammar Improves Writing." *Bad Ideas About Writing*. Edited by Cheryl E. Ball and Drew M. Loewe. Morgantown, WV: West Virginia University Libraries, Digital Publishing Institute, 2017. CC-BY.

CHAPTER 3.3: GENRES TO PRACTICE.

Here is a chart of medium-sized projects that will help you practice creating/composing various genres. Your instructor may assign one or more from each category.[78] Brief introductions to the genres follow this chapter, in their own individual chapters, and they contain student examples!

Category A: Brief & Correspondence-Based Genres	Details of Medium Project	Criteria = At a minimum, include the following:
Blog	Create five blog entries revolving around your life.	1) Five quality entries of content; 2) five accompanied pieces of info: charts, memes, images.
Email	Write an email to the president of our college, letting them know the benefits and pitfalls of attending NDSCS.	1) Some sort of structure: intro, body, conclusion; 2) Three benefits/pitfalls (total) with details; 3) A "professional"[79] tone
Letter	Write a complaint letter or complimentary letter to a company of your choice.	1) Structure: opening, body, closing/signature; 2) Three reasons - with evidence - as to why you're writing; 3) A "professional" tone
Memo	Compose a memo that is an introduction of yourself.	Follow the example in the chapter. 1) Block of info at top; 2) 3-5 Headers of details.
Text Message	<insert student-created medium project>	<insert student-created medium project>
Tweet	Head to Twitter (or Pinterest or anywhere actual tweets or screenshots of tweets exist) and dig out three (3) that you want to analyze.	In your analysis, your response to these three tweets should be your own tweets; yes, make sure you do not go over 280 characters in each tweet.
Category B: Personal Genres	Details of Medium Project	Criteria = At a minimum, include the following:
Obituary	Write your own obituary. Think about what might be said about your life. {OR, if	1) Content in third person; 2) life details; 3) chronological order.

---

[78] Students might want to jump ahead into those chapter of genres they think they'd like to practice JUST TO check out the samples and formatting, etc.

[79] What is a professional tone?

	that's too dark, write the obituary of your favorite character from TV or a movie or book.}	
Memoir	Write about a specific event in your life up to this point. Please make sure you have a lot of details and that it doesn't span more than a day or two.	1) Structure of paragraphs; 2) content FULL of details; 3) snapshot of life; 4) reflection (optional).
Multi-Genre	Create a multi-genre piece about yourself that answers the question: "Who Are You?"	Include the use of 5 different genres.
Profile	Compose a small interview-based pieces about someone you know. You should interview the person over the phone, text, or email. Ask interesting questions; get them to tell stories.	Details on: 1) Appearance; 2) Background/heritage; 3) Personality. Also: 4) Use quotes from interview; 5) Make sure you have written about them in a way that lets us into who they really are.
Category C: Technical Genres	Details of Medium Project	Criteria = At a minimum, include the following:
Business Plan	Create a Business Plan based on a company you'd like to own in the future.	1) Executive Summary; 2) Products and Services; 3) Market analysis; 4) Sales and Marketing Strategy; 5) Operations and Management; 6) Finance.
"How To"	Write a how to guide similar to the example in the chapter. Ideas: "How to be a Gearhead," or "How to be a Nurse," or "How to be a Typical College Student."	Use these headers: 1) Intro; 2)Materials Needed, and 3) Steps (with any warnings).
Proposal	This deals with College Redesign[80]. You will propose a total redesign of one aspect of your college experience. This might include: the academic calendar, grading &	Use these headers: 1) Intro; 2) Audience; 3) The End Product; 4) Costs and Supplies; 5) Tentative Schedule. Also: 6) Make sure you outline a redesign you think would benefit students: Get creative but make a good-faith effort to propose

[80] This assignment was developed for the class Punk and the Making of Self at Ithaca College, Fall 2016, by Dr. S. Alexander Reed: http://salexanderreed.com/ Licensed CC-BY-NC-SA.

	assessment, faculty & hiring, residential life, housing/food, what a degree is...	something that you might actually like to see happen.
Report	Compose a progress report on how you are doing in this class or any other class.	1) Block of info at top; 2) Review of work completed; 3) Problems; 4) Work remaining; 5) Conclusion. See example in chapter.
Resume	Create your own visual resume from your text-based one. Check out the example in the chapter!	Before and After, showcasing the change from very textual to very visual; use at least three (3) creative elements: images, borders, complimentary typefaces and sizes, white space usage, etc....
Category D: Creative Genres	**Details of Medium Project**	**Criteria = At a minimum, include the following:**
Essay	A: PURPLE SQUIRREL. Are you a purple squirrel? This term is being used to describe students who are able to do the technical skills of a job while utilizing soft skills like written and verbal communication, critical thinking and problem solving, customer service, conflict resolution, etc. B: FUTURE COMMUNITY. How do you think the community you live in can benefit from your education when you graduate from this college? C: DIFFERENT RACE/GENDER. How would your life be different had you been born into a different ethnicity/race/gender?	1) Some sort of structure: intro, body, conclusion (does not have to follow the five-paragraph essay model!) AND 2) three pieces of evidence or three stories to explain your point, etc.
List Essay	Compose a humorous essay titled "10 Ways You Know You're in a Bad Relationship or Friendship."	1) List of 10; 2) Each item should have an explanation; 3) Make sure it's humorous. Follow the list format found in the chapter's sample.

Manifesto	Write up your very own manifesto.	1) Some sort of structure (intro, body, conclusion); 2) Focus/thesis; 3) Three precepts with details; Passionate/persuasive language
Meme	Create a meme of yourself or your pet.	Meme's message should be about college.
Poetry	Write a free verse poem about NDSCS. Rhyming is not required.	1) Include 10 lines of description so we can "experience poetry through our eyes or our ears." 2) The poem should also "excite pleasure, but it can also reflect sorrow or regret."

Category E: Argumentative & Research Genres	Details of Medium Project	Criteria = At a minimum, include the following:
Annotated Bibliography	Create an annotated bibliography capturing the summaries of three sources related to your field of study OR related to a hobby of yours. (Click here for an example.)	1) Three alphabetical sources; 2) three quality summaries, and 3) three detailed citations.
Commentary	If you would like to compose a literary commentary, use our textbook as the piece to analyze. At the minimum, include the following criteria: For a social commentary, here's your topic = When it comes to the future: Are Americans getting smarter, or the opposite? How do you know either way?	1) Some sort of structure: intro, body, conclusion; 2) An argumentative thesis; 3) Three pieces of evidence that back your thesis.
Review	Compose a movie, book, or TV show review. Gather basic facts about the book/movie/TV show and take notes.	1) Start with a compelling fact or opinion on the book/movie; 2) Give a clear, well-established opinion early on; 3) Move beyond the obvious plot analysis; 4) Bring your review full-circle in the ending.
Argument	Compose an argument that answers the following: Do grades in any course reflect who you are as a student or how much you have	1) An argumentative thesis; 2) Three pieces of evidence that back your thesis; 3) One quality source integrated into the text and cited correctly at the end.

learned? Think on any college or high school course you've taken – did that letter grade reflect what you learned? Why or why not? Do letter grades represent a student's ability or intelligence? Your answers to these questions will become an argument. Some sort of structure: intro, body, conclusion

W▵TSKY ✓

@gwatsky

always work on two projects at once. that way you can procrastinate on project A by messing around on project B, and when you get tired of project B you can waste time by working on project A. you will be twice as productive while doing nothing but procrastinate

CHAPTER 3.4: LARGE PROJECTS.

These projects may or may not be used in the composition course you are taking. Or your instructor may assign just a few. Or your instructor may give you a choice.

SDGS PROJECT

WHAT CAN YOU DO TO MAKE THE WORLD A BETTER PLACE?

<u>Goal</u>: The purpose is to ask WHAT you can do to make the world a better place. Link this to your future job/career, if you'd like. Consider the SDGs (https://sdgs.un.org/goals), by the United Nations Development Program, as a starting point for the issues facing the world.

Create a video, slide presentation, or infographic (or choose another medium) in which you research one way to make the world a better place. At a minimum, the project will include:

- Introduction with two headers: Background on Topic & Research Question
- Quality interviews & their summaries conducted by the student or others.
- Quality surveys & their summaries conducted by the student or others.
- Implementation of student personal experience with topic.
- Quality content and a solid structure (intro, body, conclusion) that answers: What, Who, How, Where, and When.
- All sources cited correctly in the text and at the end of the project.

Students will choose a research question & attempt to answer it using primary sources. Primary research is first-hand info like interviews (conducted by the student or others), surveys, personal experiences, etc.

- Brainstorm.
  - A research question that is interesting to you.
  - Who could you interview?
  - Who could you survey?
- Read the Research Chapter in our textbook.
- Begin to collect research.
  - Conduct your own interview or seek out experts who've already been interviewed (TED, YouTube).
  - Create your own survey using Google Forms or Survey Monkey (or use email, text, social media) OR seek our surveys completed by others on your topic using the resources found on the campus library site OR Google Scholar.
- Follow the writing process phases to draft, revise, and edit. This is optional.
- Submit the final project draft & fill out the self-assessment, if necessary.

Brainstorming:
- How does recycling help the earth? What more can I be doing? (SDG #12)
- How can free college programs nationwide help to eliminate poverty? (SDG #4)
- How can Z-Degrees assist all students in learning, persisting through college, and graduating? (SDG #4)
- [Architectural Drafting Student] Could I design some kind of living community off-the-grid that assists homeless people? (SDG #11)
- [Auto Body Student] What technologies exist to lower emissions? (SDG #7)
- [Dental Student] How can dental hygiene contribute to the SDG #3: Good Health and Well-Being?
- If you plan to become a parent, you might ask: "What are the best parenting philosophies?"

TEXTBOOK TWEAK

Goal: **Imagine a textbook written by students and for students!** What if we threw out any textbook for this class! What could the textbook look like with total student control? Create a chapter for that sort of textbook that doesn't exist yet.

Create a video, slide presentation, or infographic (or choose another medium) in which you create a student-friendly chapter for an imaginary textbook. At a minimum, the project will include:
- A new chapter.
- An accompanied visual aid.
- Facts.

STEPS:

Step 1: Brainstorm what you either think is missing from the current textbook for this class and compose that chapter OR ask yourself what current chapter needs to be completely tweaked and revise that one heavily.
- Feel free to be silly or cuss or use stories to talk about the genre.

Step 2: Compose the chapter with at least one visual aid (chart, meme, picture) that is openly licensed (possible sites to check out: Unsplash, Shutterstock, Getty Images, Pexels, Freepik, etc.).

Step 3: Double-check all facts and information you use. Cite information that doesn't come from your head (and/or use footnotes).

Step 4: Submit a final draft before the deadline and self-assess your project.

MORE BRAINSTORMING...
- Should there be a "history of writing" chapter?
- What about a chapter on swear words and their histories?
- What about a chapter on slang?
- Why isn't there a chapter on AAVE/Ebonics?
- Should there be a chapter on note-taking?
- Are all the genres and strategies for writing covered?

PROJECT PLAYLIST

Goal: Students will choose 5-10 media works that demonstrate who they are as people.

Create a slide presentation or infographic in which you create a playlist of media works that showcase who you are as a person. At a minimum, the project will include:
- Seven slides.
  - Cover page.
  - Table of Contents.
  - Five slides of media.
- An annotation or summary of each media work.
- A picture (one preferably in the Creative Commons) of the media work with a citation of where the picture came from.

THE UNESSAY

The **Un-Essay**[81] is an assignment that allows the ultimate in creativity. It asks you to focus solely on your intellectual interests and passions. In an Un-Essay you choose your own topic, present it any way you please, and are evaluated on how well it all fits together and if it's effective.

CHOOSE YOUR OWN TOPIC

The Un-Essay allows you to write about anything you want provided you are able to associate your topic with the subject matter of the course. The only requirements are that your treatment of the topic be compelling and effective: that is to say presented in a way that leaves the reader thinking that you are being accurate, interesting, and as complete and/or convincing as your subject allows.

PRESENT IT ANY WAY YOU PLEASE

There are also no formal requirements. Your essay can be written in five paragraphs, or three, or twenty-six. If you decide you need to cite something, you can do that any way you want. If you want to use lists, use lists. If you want to write in the first person, write in the first person. If you prefer to present the whole thing as a video, present it as a video. Use slang. Or don't. Sentence fragments if you think that would be effective. In other words, in an Un-Essay you have complete freedom of form: you can use whatever style of writing, presentation, citation,… even media you want. What is important is that the format and presentation you do use helps rather than hinders your explanation of the topic.

BE EVALUATED ON HOW EFFECTIVE YOU ARE

If Un-Essays can be about anything and there are no restrictions on format and presentation, how are they "graded"? Well, they are "graded" by the student; they will assess how well it all fits together, and whether the project is effective.

---

[81] This content comes from Daniel Paul O'Donnell - https://people.uleth.ca/~daniel.odonnell/Teaching/the-unessay. Unless otherwise noted, the non-negotiated licence for all work on this site is Creative Commons Attribution-NonCommercial-ShareAlike 3.0 Unported License.

PROJECT STATEMENT[82]
You must write a statement that explains what you did, why you did it, and how you went about producing, and the sources you used for the Un-Essay.

SELF-ASSESSMENT QUESTIONS
1. What did you learn?
2. What challenges did you face while completing this assignment?
3. How did you overcome these challenges?
4. How effective or successful do you think you were with your final product?
5. What do you think you could have done differently?

THE FAKE COMPANY PROJECT

Create a slide presentation or infographic in which you showcase specific pieces of a fake company you[83] may like to start one day; this needs to be an original idea. At a minimum, the project will include:
- The company's mission statement.
- The company's logo, motto, letterhead, and business card.
- Advertisements – both to customers and future employees.
- Pie charts of the company's monthly or yearly income and expenses.
- A progress report.
- A condensed business plan.

THE SELF-IMPROVEMENT PROJECT

Create a slide presentation, or infographic, or choose another medium in which you report on a 2-week experiment done on yourself. At a minimum, the project will include:
- One narrowed experiment; here are possible categories:
  - Spiritual: meditate, read up on a new religion, etc.
  - Academic: improve study habits, decrease procrastination, etc.
  - Physical: strength training, flexibility, endurance, drink more water, etc.
  - Financial: save money, learn about the stock market, etc.
- Research on what the experts say about what can be achieved in 2 weeks within that category.
- Then create one goal for the 2 weeks.
  - Possible example for spiritual = Meditate 5x a day.
  - Possible example for financial = Save
- A log of information displaying the 2-week experiment.
- A summary of the experiment.
- Conclusion.

---

[82] **CARA OCOBOCK, PH.D.** - https://sites.nd.edu/cara-ocobock/un-essay/
[83] You might be allowed to complete this in groups of three or less.

THE OPEN PROJECT

You might spend some part of the semester working on an open project. This planning document will give you the tools you need to guide your work.

TOOLS AND MEDIA

Your project can take any number of forms, such as a new chapter for the textbook, a "how to" guide, a novella, an original website on a certain topic, children's book, graphic novel, flash fiction challenge, a research project, an argumentative paper, an infographic, a video, or a set of Google Slides or a Powerpoint that tells a story.

END PRODUCT

My open project will be: _____.

At a minimum,
you should create a high-quality project and design everything yourself.

BRIEF PROPOSED TIMELINE

Fill out this proposed timeline outlining your plans for this final project:

- ____<date>____ - Phase 1 of Writing Process (Brainstorming & Outline) completed; I will _____.
- ____<date>____ - Phase 2 of Writing Process (Draft and Revision) completed. I will _____.
- ____<date>____ - Phases 3 and 4 (Proofreading/Editing/Submission) completed. I will _____.
- Please consider using a tutor or Grammarly/Hemingway App or a nerdy classmate.

PEER REVIEW/WORKSHOP

On ____<date>____, you will share a draft of your work [online]. My draft will include _____. I will offer WWW/TAG feedback to my peers. And, of course, I will chat with Sybil via email or over the phone/Zoom if I want to chat and get additional feedback at any point.

SHARING YOUR WORK

You should consider publishing your work to the web or in a future edition of this book. The audience for your work shouldn't just be Sybil or the members of our class, but rather the public, your friends, and your family.

I PROMISE

I promise to trust myself, my classmates, and to do as best I can on this project. I am capable, creative, and willing to engage with the material necessary to complete this project. Initial here: _____

ULTIMATE STUDENT CHOICE PROJECT

Place a checkmark next to the option you'd like to complete. You can change your mind at any point, but that does put more stress on yourself, so keep that in mind.

_Option 1: Student-Created. You will proposal a project to Sybil no later than Week 14. Please use the planning pieces of "The Open Project."	_Option 2: Workplace.[84] You will complete everything in Chapter 3.7.	_Option 3: Reading. You will complete 10/30 reading responses in Chapter 3.6.
_Option 4: Creation. You will create questions, activities, and/or exercises for 5 chapters that do not have any right now.	_Option 5: Visual. You will create visuals for 5 chapters that need them. These should be original and not copied from Google, etc.	_Option 6: Random. You will complete HALF of the prompts in Chapter 3.5 OR ALL of the prompts in Chapter 3.8.

FUTURE LIFE PROJECT

Create a slide presentation, or infographic, or choose another medium in which you report on your future life possibilities. At a minimum, the project will include:

- A cover page and table of contents.
- Bulleted List of Possible Incomes in 3-5 different places.
- A Screenshot of a list of Job Responsibilities/Qualifications for the job you want.
- Bulleted List of 3-5 Companies that you could work for.
- Images of 3-5 Places you could live.
- A Valid and Detailed Pie Chart showing the breakdown of spending once you have the job you want.
- Screenshots* or citations of sources = where you found all of your information (web sites, names of newspapers, people you interviewed, etc.).
- Reflection: summarize what you want your future life to look like – think 5-10 years into the future and give your readers a snapshot of what your daily life looks like. What are you doing, where are you living, what are you living in, who are you surrounded by, are you happy, etc.

*SCREENSHOTS:
When you are on a website that you will take information from, hit the Print Screen button on the keyboard, if you are on a PC. With a Mac, use Shift + Command + 4.

---

[84] This one is "perfect" for students who are into technical writing and/or are majoring in technical fields.

CHAPTER 3.5: SEVENTEEN PROMPTS.

1. Be bad: Write a bad essay. Attempt writing badly.
2. Dear "Dead Person." Write a letter to someone who has passed away.
3. "Watch Your Language." What are the words you love, or the phrases you wish would come back in fashion?
4. Inventory: What are your favorite things? Favorite movies, musicians, stores, foods, etc.
5. Address your people: "My fellow classmates, …"
6. Write two sides of one story. Think "he said – she said."
7. Speak Your Truth: Give us 5-10 of some of your own unique beliefs.
8. Dear Abby: Write an essay modeled on an advice column.
9. Examine Your Past: Find an old note or journal entry (or email message) & analyze it.
10. Show Them Some Love: Tell us who your friends are and why they are a part of your life.
11. Blow Your Budget: You've come into ten million dollars – How do you spend it? Be specific!
12. My Family: Write about the members of your family. Describe each person.
13. New Student Questions: If there was a new student in class and you could only ask that person three questions to get to know them, what would you ask them? WHY?
14. The Musical You: What is the soundtrack to your life? Tell us what your three favorite songs are right now and why.
15. Body Parts: If a part of your body (or parts) could talk to you, which part would it be & what would it say?
16. Take anything you've written in the last few months and do a remix = switch out half of the words with their synonyms. How does the piece change?
17. Write a letter to your younger self. What would you tell yourself at age 10 or 15?

---

[85] Your instructor may decide that these will extend beyond "10-minute prompts" into a full-blown project.
[86] I found these so very long ago, and if anyone knows who created the list, please shoot me their name so I can give them credit.

CHAPTER 3.6: THIRTY WRITING & READING ACTIVITIES.

Teachers may assign these activities FOLLOWING any sort of reading that was required for the course.

OPTION 1: Flickr/Pixlr Image Creation
Idea: This activity visualizes the reading. You will find an image that connects to the quote/statement you find most interesting in the chapter you just read. Using the Creative Commons area of Flickr.com or Unsplash, you'll save the image and add text (or a quote) by using Pixlr.com. From there, you could upload the image to an LMS or insert it into a document to be handed in. Or, hell, maybe you'll just email it to whoever needs to see it.

OPTION 2: Facebook Status(es)
Idea: You will create a Facebook status of the topic or person in the reading. Perhaps there will be comments to that status by other people in the reading.

OPTION 3: Top Ten
Idea: You would rank something in the reading for class. If the chapter is about blogs, maybe you would rank the top ten blogs you might read.

OPTION 4: Twitter Sitter
Idea: In 280 characters or less, you will sum up what you read.

OPTION 5: Text Type-Up
Idea: You might learn the best through repetition, and yet don't want to mark up your paper textbooks. So, this activity asks you to type (or write) up a piece of the reading you'd like to respond to. After typing or writing up the piece, you can then circle things you don't understand or really find interesting.

OPTION 6: Animoto Video Trailer
Idea: Just like how movies have previews, maybe discussions should too? This activity asks you to create a trailer or preview of the upcoming discussion by reading and then putting related images and text into Animoto.com. Their 30-second videos are free and easy to use. From there, you could upload the URL to an LMS to be viewed in class. {Animoto.com}

OPTION 7: Prezi/PPT
Idea: In order for you to prep for the upcoming discussion of the reading, you should create parts of the possible discussion by putting together a piece such as a PowerPoint slide (or slides) or Prezi presentation. You could then upload those Prezis/PPTs to a specific area in the LMS in order for the instructor to pop them up on the big screen in class.

OPTION 8: Visual Definition

Idea: Many of us naturally increase our vocabulary by reading, so this activity asks you to pick a specific number of words from the chapter to create visual definitions of. Each slide = new word made visual with images, stories, quotes from the reading, definitions, etc.

OPTION 9: Create a Quiz

Idea: In order to create a quality quiz, you need to know the material. So, you should create quizzes from everything you read (if you have time); the quiz or quizzes could contain multiple-choice questions, T/F, and even short answer questions. The quizzes, then, could be exchanged with classmates?

OPTION 10: The Crossword Puzzle

Idea: You would use an online crossword puzzle-making site to create a crossword related to the reading material. {http://puzzle-maker.com/[87] or some other web site?}

OPTION 11: (Fake) Interview

Idea: You could either interview someone about what you've just read, or you could create a document which shows a fake interview with the author about the piece. Sometimes, creating fake content is just as difficult as "real" content.

OPTION 12: Survey the Masses

Idea: After you read, you could conduct a survey of those around you (f2f or email or Facebook) about the topic(s) covered in the piece.

OPTION 13: Weird Poetry

Idea: After reading, you could reconstruct parts of the text into chunks. Slices of the text, fragments, put into poetic bite size bits.

OPTION 14: Dear Author

Idea: You could write an actual letter to the author of the piece.

OPTION 15: Jeopardy

Idea: While reading, create Jeopardy questions or maybe a whole game with points assigned (200 level questions versus 400 level questions). You could play the game with classmate in or out of class together.

OPTION 16: Do you know your ABCs?

Idea: Use all 26 letters to find things in the reading that pertain to each letter. (There may be an example of this at the end of this section?)

OPTION 17: The 5x5

Idea: Whatever you are reading, find 5 quotes and then 5 terms and create a story out of them.

OPTION 18: Mad Libs

---

[87] In existence as of November 2021.

Idea: You could create a mad lib, or a few, (Google that term if you've never used a Mad Lib before) based on the reading.

OPTION 19: The Kevin Bacon-ator
Idea: Connect two unlike things (genres, chapters, topics, authors, etc.) with the 6 (or is it 7) Steps to Kevin Bacon idea.

OPTION 20: Fake Book Citations
Idea: While reading, you could create fake book citations for books that would relate to the material in a serious or fun way.

OPTION 21: Factoid/Something Cool
Idea: Search the text for someone or something. From there, you could find something cool or some factoid about that topic. Ex: If you are reading about World War II, you could look online for something interesting about the fashions of the time or what people drove (if you are into fashion/cars, for example).

OPTION 22: Artistic Summary/Pictionary
Idea: Draw out what happened in the reading. It could lead into a game of Pictionary with classmates.

OPTION 23: Multi-Genre
Idea: Find multiple genres that connect to the topic(s)/theme(s) in the reading or chapter. Ex: Finding a cartoon and poem and meme about BLOGS.

OPTION 24: The Comic Strip
Idea: Using www.makebeliefscomix.com[88] (or paper & pen), you could create a comic strip based on a theme or some dialogue that occurs in the reading. This will add a bit of humor to any subject.

OPTION 25: Dear Abby Advice
Idea: Mimic a "Dear Abby" column that is related to the piece that you just read.

OPTION 26: Translation Nation
Idea: Take a paragraph from the reading. Translate it into how a politician would say it. THEN translate it into how a child or elderly person would say it.

OPTION 27: Teeny Tiny Talk
Idea: Find an image on Flickr.com of two or more people. Add bubbles for conversation using Pixlr.com. Connect what you read for class to the conversation. There is a low-tech sample image below. If you can draw, recreate this on paper with pen/pencil.

---

[88] In existence as of November 2021.

OPTION 28: Activity Exchange
Idea: Create your own post-reading activity. Exchange it with a classmate and complete theirs.

OPTION 29: Fake Ad
Idea: Create an ad for something sold in the chapter or reading.

OPTION 30: Timeline
Idea: Create a timeline of the reading.

WANT.AN.EXAMPLE?
WANT.A.SAMPLE?

OPTION 16 Example:

What if, as humans, we are the things being "read." What nuggets would a person take away from reading me (Sybil/creator of this book)?

"SYBIL: AN ALPHABETICAL JOURNEY TO THE PERSON I HAVE BECOME."

A = Aquarius. "While Aquarians are generally sympathetic and compassionate, they like it when things go their own quirky way. Some might call their behavior eccentric (and they would be right), but when you consider that the Aquarian's heart is truly in the right place, a few oddities should be overlooked." [www.astrology.com]

B = Beck. Blasphemy. Bicycles.

C = Classes Taught. Classes taught: (middle-school) student-taught 8th grade English at the West Fargo Middle School; (high school) taught Freshmen English, Junior English, Senior English, and Publications (yearbook/newspaper) at Battle Lake High School; (university) taught College Composition I: English 110 & College Composition II: English 120 at NDSU; (community colleges) taught Professional Communications and Fundamentals of English at Aakers Business College; taught College Composition I: English 110 at Northwest Tech in Detroit Lakes; (currently) Technical Communications: English 105, College Composition I: English 110, College Composition II: English 120, World Masterpieces: English 240, and Intro to Creative Writing: English 211.

D = Drafting and Design. "D'oh!" – Homer Simpson.

E = Ellen DeGeneres. "Today I'd like to talk about librarians. I don't know how many of them watch my show. If they do, they probably watch my show while reading or working on the Dewey Decimal System. They probably don't watch much TV at all. They just wait for the transcripts. If they do watch the show, they probably keep the sound turned down and put their fingers up to their mouths and say, "Shhhhhhhh" every time the audience laughs."

F = *Fahrenheit 451*. The f-bomb.

G = "Growth-seeking individual."[89]

H = Hell. I joke about probably ending up in hell. "If you are going through hell, keep going." Winston Churchill said that.

I = Intolerant of lactose.

J = Joyce. It's the best "old lady name" ever. My sister and I use it as an expletive. Jeep.

K = Karma. "The total effect of a person's actions and conduct during the successive phases of the person's existence, regarded as determining the person's destiny." [Dictionary.com]

L = Lexicography. Lady Gaga.

M = Mark, my dad. Magazines. Marathons.

N = Numbers. 7. 3. 33. 47. First off, when I go places, and a tip is needed to be figured in, I like to round up to odd numbers. I love spending $17, for example. I feel like it's good luck. Fourteen dollars? Na.

O = I am an optimist, and I am the oldest of four.

---

[89] The best compliment Sybil's ever received from a colleague.

P = Priebe. Project Runway. Paddleboarding. *Parks & Rec.*

Q = Quit. Quit worrying about my weight. Quit this. Quit that.

R = Raining days are the best. I love clouds and not having to squint. Plus, the smell is a bonus.

S = Shopping, *Sex & The City*, Sarah Jessica Parker, Shoes. Sushi. Sadie.

T = I used to be a tomboy, and I loved the sport of tennis.

U = Ungrading.

V = Volleyball. And Volkswagen.

W = Weblog. "Be the Blog: Myself as a Test Subject." Since throwing myself into the "blogosphere" in 2002, I've been blogging privately and publicly as well as used class blogs in my Composition/Literature courses. I've researched the pros and cons of blogging; dissecting student blogging has become my odd passion. I've happily annoyed other academics (and, yes, even non-academics) with my blogging knowledge/experience for quite some time, so why stop now? As an eternal optimist, I have a few recommendations for why students and teachers should jump on the blogging wagon.

X = Check mark. I like to make lists and check items off one at a time.

Y = Yoda.

Z = Zephyr, which is the western wind. I've been fascinated by meteorology for a long time. Looking at doppler radars and figuring out what will come to us from the west, from the Rockies.

CHAPTER 3.7: WORKPLACE EXERCISES

HYPOTHETICAL EMAILS. One of the following may be chosen by the instructor:

a) Your proposal went through introducing a new company rule, and now you are the proud owner of this new rule. Please send three different email messages to three different audiences introducing and explaining the new rule. Each message should be 100+ words.

b) There was an incident report completed regarding someone getting hurt in your company. You need to send the incident report to three different audiences, summarizing what happened to them in three different ways. Each message should be 100+ words.

c) You have a workplace message that needs to be distributed company-wide; however, some people might not take the message well. Write three different email messages to the three different audiences that need to hear the message. Each message should be 100+ words.

HYPOTHETICAL SITUATION.

CREATE A HYPOTHETICAL SITUATION ABOUT YOUR FUTURE WORKPLACE. Write up your own hypothetical situation that you will exchange with a classmate. The situation should be realistic, and the end product is required to contain some sort of writing. **Make sure the situation answers what, where, when, why, and how questions.** Here are some examples to help you brainstorm your own scenario:
- Your boss sends out an email, and you see a few spelling errors in the email. Do you bring it to your boss's attention or ignore it?
- What if a co-worker brings up the email and mocks the boss, saying the boss is an idiot? What is your communication to the co-worker?

CHAPTER 3.8: EFFS

THE FIVE WORDS

In addition to writing and reading in most college composition courses, the five words that may be at the core of the class (or college and life in general, really) are autonomy, empathy and sympathy, and creativity and problem-solving. Please write 100 words for each word, giving your definition(s) of the word and experience(s) you've had with it.

FOUR FICTION PROMPTS

A. One day, you notice there's a new key on your keychain.

B. And then they said, "You did what?" "It wasn't as bad as last time, I swear."

C. There's an urban legend that's been circulating for years, about a taxi cab that doesn't take you where you want to go, but where you need to go. One night, you step into this cab.

D. The (Odd) Bodyguard: Write a short story from the point-of-view of a character who works as a personal bodyguard. The catch? This character looks nothing like a fighter. Double catch? This character possesses an ability that makes their job very easy.

FAMOUS PARENTS

If you could have any two famous people as your parents, who would you choose and why? Respond in 500+ words (break down each person into 250+ if you want). Feel free to go the nontraditional route and have two women as parents, etc.

FIVE BUTTONS

RED BUTTON: Turns you invisible, including your clothes.
BLUE BUTTON: Gives you the ability to fly.
YELLOW BUTTON: Gives you the ability to read people's thoughts.
GREY BUTTON: Allow you to lift any objects with your mind.
PINK BUTTON: Allows you the gift to heal any wound, whether it be yours or others'.

WHICH BUTTON - choose just one - DO YOU HIT TODAY AND WHY? Respond in 250-500 words.

CHAPTER 3.9: INDIVIDUALITY

Create your own cover for a CD. Use Flickr.com (or Unsplash) and Pixlr.com or go the low-tech route and use markers + paper.

PERSONAL SYLLABUS

HUM 101 = CLASS ON HOW TO BECOME ALMOST AS INTERESTING AS I AM

INSTRUCTOR (your name): _____
READING LIST #1 _____
READING LIST #2 _____
READING LIST #3 _____
READING LIST #4 _____
READING LIST #5 _____
LISTENING LIST #1 _____
LISTENING LIST #2 _____
LISTENING LIST #3 _____
LISTENING LIST #4 _____
LISTENING LIST #5 _____
VIEWING LIST #1 _____
VIEWING LIST #2 _____
VIEWING LIST #3 _____
VIEWING LIST #4 _____
VIEWING LIST #5 _____
CENTRAL EXPERIENCE (TO BE COMPLETED BY AGE 12):
CENTRAL EXPERIENCE (TO BE COMPLETED BY AGE 17):
CREATIVE PROJECT:
HAVE SUBSTANTIALLY DIFFERENT BELIEFS THAN YOUR PARENTS DO ABOUT:
IN THIS CLASS, YOU ARE NOT ALLOWED TO:
THE BEST WAY TO GET ON MY GOOD SIDE:
THE QUICKEST WAY TO PISS ME OFF:
EXTRA CREDIT WILL BE GIVEN FOR:
HAVING TAKEN THIS CLASS, YOU'LL BE PREPARED FOR A FUTURE DOING...

THE PILLS

YELLOW PILL: Allows you to read and search minds of people. Also allows you to turn off a person's mind, putting them into a coma.
GREEN PILL: Allows you to shape-shift into any animal.
BLUE PILL: Allows you to teleport to any area, but you can not time travel.
ORANGE PILL: Gives to the ability to master any sport or job or activity in seconds.
RED PILL: Gives you super speed and rapid regeneration.

PINK PILL: Makes any person you touch fall in love with you. The effect can be reversed by retouching the person.
GREY PILL: Gives you the ability to control any electronic machine with your mind.

WHICH OF THESE 3 PILLS DO YOU NOT WANT TO DIGEST EVER AND WHY? Respond in 250-500 words.

STUDENT-CREATED OPTIONS[90]

	8am Student-Creations:
	Create a Venn Diagram comparing & contrasting two things we've read for this class during this semester.
	Illustrate (draw pictures of, etc.) one of the readings we did for this class.
	Create a 6-sentence story about what you plan to do over the upcoming holiday break. Then write that story in texting language.
	Read: "12 Things that Back to the Future Promised We'd Have by 2015" on buzzfeed.com; after reading, write a reaction to what you feel we are falling behind on, and if you think those inventions will exist in the year 2015.
	Write a rap or poetry slam based on any of the readings we've done for class this semester.
	1pm Student-Creations:
	Pick a famous person you admire & write a 50+ worded paragraph on why you admire them.
	Choose a piece of art. Critique the piece you have chosen. Answer both of these questions: What do you like about it? What would you change about it?
	Nifty Fifty: Summarize this semester in exactly 50 words.
	Story Time: Create a 5+ page children's book about anything we've read this semester.
	Pick a fairy tale. Change the ending of it.
	Pick a word at least 7 letters in length. Write a continuation of the story, each sentence starting with a letter from the word. For example: Confusion = First sentence starts with "C," second with "O," etc.
	Interview Yourself. Ask yourself 5 questions and answer them.
	Choose any one of these sentences as your first and finish the story: (1) An asteroid was heading towards Earth… (2) Let me tell you a little Christmas Story… (3) This one time in English class…
	Pick a singer/band/actor. Make a story out of their song titles or movies. 10+ sentences. Example: "Will Smith grew up in the Wild Wild West. When he was 18, he decided to leave on Independence Day. He went to NYC for his Pursuit of Happiness."
	3pm Student-Creations:
	Create a tweet as a political leader that would hurt your chances to get re-elected. Then create 2 subsequent tweets to try and apologize.
	Write a radio message selling a new product!

[90] Collected December 2014.

	Mini-Media Paper = Respond to: Could you make it through a media fast if it was a day in length? This means no media (internet, TV, radio, etc.) for 24hours. Why or why not?

DIY

<Feel free to create your own prompt and share it with the teacher; it may end up in a future edition of this book!>

LYRICS

Use the lyrics of a favorite song to write an essay on a topic completely different than the topic of the song. Additional words may be used, but every word from the lyrics must be in the essay.

VENT SESSION

Think of something you hate. Something you cannot stand; something that makes you extremely angry. Now, write "On" in front of that something and you have the title of your essay. Do not edit, do not stop to think. Just write. Example essay titles: "On Disrespecting Elders..." "On the font of Times New Roman..."

IF...

- If you could have one superpower, what would it be? Write a few paragraphs explaining what the superpower is, why you would like to have it, and what you would do with this new power. How would your life change if you had this superpower?
- If you could be any age at all, how old would you be (older or younger)? Write about why you would like to be this age and what you would do.
- If you were going to be stranded on a deserted island and could take three items with you, what three items would you take and why? The three items have to fit in an ordinary backpack. Describe each item fully and tell why you want each one.
- If you could go back in time and re-experience an event in your life, what would it be. Would you go back to change an event that happened or to re-experience a happy time? Or something else?
- If I Were a Teacher: Write a few paragraphs on what you would do if you were a teacher for a day. What subjects would you teach and how would you teach them?
- If you could give yourself a new name, what would it be? Write about why you chose this new name and how it might change your life.

 **Kashana**
@kashanacauley

Emails just aren't safe. We should hide state secrets deep in the story parts of recipe blogs.

1:26 PM · 11 Oct 16

391 RETWEETS   **1,150** LIKES

CHAPTER 4: GENRES.

The following genres are listed and explained in alphabetical order. What are genres? Well, just like in music, they are categories. In this case, they are categories of writing where the audiences can vary as well as the content and structure. Think of techno or rap or pop music; the content of all of those music genres is different than country music, yes? But it's all under the umbrella of music.

And yes, there is sometimes overlap between writing genres just like there is with musical genres.

POP QUIZ ON GENRES

Your friend, Noor, has been in a romantic relationship with Amor for the past two years. A few months ago, Noor moved to another city and, after trying to have a long-distance relationship, has decided to break up with Amor. Noor wants to break up in writing because they are scared that they won't be able to go through with it in person (or over the phone) because Amor will talk them out of it. Noor still loves Amor and wants this to be as painless as possible for both of them.

What genre of writing should Noor use to break up with Amor?

Instagram / Social Media
Handwritten Letter
Report
Email
Text
Memo
Tweet

Whatever your response/answer is, it shows that you already are quite skilled at using rhetoric[92] and genre. You may not believe this, but your brain conducted a instinctive rhetorical and genre calculation to come to your decision. It may have only taken a second or two, but you and your brain sorted through all of the (implicit) elements of rhetoric to make a pretty solid decision on which was the most appropriate genre.

QUESTIONS:

- Why did you choose the genres you chose for this break-up message?
- Why would some of those genres not work for this situation?
- Which genres from that list are you not familiar with right now?

---

[91] Rhetoric and Genre: You've Got This! (Even if You Don't Think You Do) by Liza Long; Amy Minervini; and Joel Gladd is licensed under a Creative Commons Attribution-NonCommercial 4.0 International License, except where otherwise noted.
[92] According to *Merriam Webster's Dictionary*, Rhetoric is **"the art of speaking or writing effectively**: such as. a : the study of principles and rules of composition formulated by critics of ancient times. b : the study of writing or speaking as a means of communication or persuasion."

ANNOTATED BIBLIOGRAPHY

The annotated bibliography[93] is one of the possible first steps to writing a successful research paper. By completing an annotated bibliography, you will begin your research long before the actual research paper is due, so you can gather what is out there and filter what you want to use in your draft.

DEFINITION:

An annotation is a brief summary of a book, article, chart, visual, video or other publication. The purpose of an annotation is to describe the work in such a way that the reader can decide whether or not to read the work itself. An annotated bibliography helps the reader understand the particular usefulness of each item. The ideal annotated bibliography shows the relationships among individual items and may compare their strengths or shortcomings.

STEP-BY-STEP APPROACH TO ANNOTATING:

The following approach to annotating will help you to use your reading time to best advantage.

- Familiarize yourself with the contents of the book or article, etc.
- Read as much of the book or article (or watch the video/listen to the podcast) as is necessary to understand its content.
- Outline or make notes of the information you think should be incorporated in the annotation.
- Write a paragraph that covers the spirit of the book or article, etc. without undue emphasis on any one or more particular points. Summarize as best you can.
- Write in complete sentences.
- The most effective annotation is tightly written with succinct and descriptive wording. Annotations are short notes and are normally no more than 150 words. Brevity and clarity are the goals.
- Grab the attention of the reader at the beginning of the annotation.

---

[93] "Rhetoric and Composition/Teacher's Handbook/Teaching Annotated Bibliography." *Wikibooks, The Free Textbook Project*. 10 Aug 2016, 20:05 UTC. 10 Sep 2019, 20:24
<https://en.wikibooks.org/w/index.php?title=RhetoricandComposition/Teacher%27sHandbook/TeachingAnnotatedBibliography&oldid=3104990>.

WANT.AN.EXAMPLE?

WANT.A.SAMPLE?

DENTAL HYGIENE: PROS AND CONS BY KENDRYN[94]

Metro-Sanchez, Amber. "Why I Would Choose Dental Hygiene all Over Again."
StackPath, 21 Feb 2017, https://www.rdhmag.com/patient-care/article/16409840/why-i-would-choose-dental-hygiene-all-over-again. In this article she talks about the negativity of social media that said hygienist don't exactly love their job. One negative thing that she pointed out was it is hard to find an office that fits your personality. She also had some good points such as, being able to spend one-on one time with her patients. She says she has heard lots of interesting stories.

"Five Benefits of a Career as a Dental Hygienist - APLUS Institute." *APLUS Institute*, 18 Dec. 2018, https://aplusinstitute.ca/5-benefits-of-a-career-as-a-dental-hygienist/. In this article they talk not only about the benefits of becoming a dental hygienist but, how you will assess pain, poorly controlled diabetes, and cardiovascular disease resulting from oral inflammation. They explain how teeth can show a lot about the health of a patient.

"Pros and Cons of Being a Dental Hygienist: Complete Mobile Dentistry." *Complete Mobile Dentistry* |, 12 June 2017, https://www.completemobiledentistry.com/pros-and-cons-of-being-a-dental-hygienist/. The article talked about four positive ideas of becoming a dental hygienist. They were growing employment, great salary, minimal schooling, and flexibility. They also brought very good negative aspects too dental hygiene too including, not much of a variety, repetitive and unpleasant patients.

---

[94] This wonderful nugget was created by Kendryn in the Spring of 2021. It's licensed CC-BY-NC-SA.

Definition: A journal-style web site that lists the posts backwards with a timestamp. Some blogs are collaborative, and some are kept up by one individual.

Blogs are one of the newest genres on the scene, and they are used in teaching, the corporate world, the land of politics. If a person has a passion, and wants to openly journal about it, he/she should consider starting a blog.

Blogs are easy to create. All it takes is one idea. Anyone can do it.

HOW DO BLOGS WORK?[95]

Blogs are created via blog hosting websites such as Blogger or WordPress. Typically, a user registers a username and password, picks a blog title and URL, and then can immediately begin his or her first post, or entry.

A post can include a combination or writing, photos, videos, links, and other embedded materials. Once the post is ready, the author can instantly publish it to the blog. Other people are then able to view the post (depending on settings--a blogger can choose to make his or her blog private, public, or shared with certain people).

Readers can subscribe to the blog and receive updates. Posts can be shared via social networking tools such as Facebook, Twitter, and Tumblr. Bloggers can also enable commenting, which means readers can write responses to blog posts that will appear along with the post for other readers to see.

All it takes is one click to post or respond to another person's blog.

CATEGORIES[96]

Here are specific sorts of blogs:
- **Political Blogs:** These blogs are often tied to a large media or news corporation.
- **Gossip Blogs:** These blogs can greatly be attributed to the popularity of Perez Hilton, a celebrity and entertainment media gossip blogger. His blog posts contain tabloid photographs of celebrities, accompanied by captions and comments. Web traffic to the often controversial and raunchy Perez Hilton site skyrocketed in 2005, prompting similar gossip blogs, such as *TMZ.com*, *Jezebel*, and the *Superficial*, to gain popularity.
- **Food Blogs:** These blogs allow foodies and aspiring chefs alike to share recipes, cooking techniques, and food porn, for others to enjoy. Food blogs serve as a sort of online cookbook for followers, often containing restaurant critiques, product reviews, and step-by-step photography for recipes.
- **Fashion Blogs:** These blogs became their own larger than life sub-community following the explosive growth of the blogosphere. Besides fashion news blogs, street style blogs have also become exceedingly popular. Many Bloggers

---

[95] "User-Generated Content in Education/Blogs." *Wikibooks, The Free Textbook Project.* 2 Apr 2018, 12:02 UTC. 7 May 2019, 19:15 <https://en.wikibooks.org/w/index.php?title=User-Generated_Content_in_Education/Blogs&oldid=3399437>. Licensed CC-BY-SA.
[96] "Social Web/Blogs." *Wikibooks, The Free Textbook Project.* 17 Dec 2014, 14:26 UTC. 8 May 2019, 19:17 <https://en.wikibooks.org/w/index.php?title=Social_Web/Blogs&oldid=2748518>. Licensed CC-BY-SA.

consider updating their blog a full-time job. These style mavens are able to earn considerable livings through advertising, selling their photos and even providing their services as photographers, stylists, and guest designers.

This is the teaching blog of Sybil (creator of this book); you can find it at: https://sybilpriebebooks.blogspot.com/

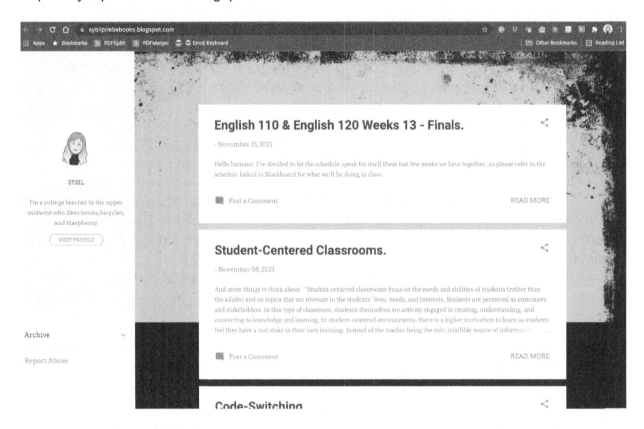

EXTRA RESOURCES

<insert links to student blogs and other great blog examples>

BUSINESS PLAN

Creating a business plan[97] will help you achieve your entrepreneurial goals. A clear and compelling business plan provides you with a guide for building a successful enterprise focused on achieving your personal and financial goals. It can also help persuade others, including banks (and other stakeholders), to invest in what you are creating.

Define your company. A business plan won't be useful until you're certain what your company exists for. What will you accomplish for others? What products and services will you produce or provide? Write down all the specific needs your company will satisfy. Potential investors need to know that your business will be meaningful and marketable to people who can use your product or service. Concentrate on the external needs your company will meet.

Choose a winning strategy. Once you've established the competitive advantage your business offers, you will be able to select the best strategy to reach your goal. How will you distinguish your product or service from others? Although there are millions of types of businesses, there are actually only a few basic strategies that can be applied to make any enterprise successful.

Design your company. Consider how will you hire and organize your workforce. By the time you've reached this stage of thinking about your potential business concept, you'll probably have a good idea of the number of people you'll need and the skills they'll require to get your enterprise up and running.

Consider the practical issues of running a business. Think about your role as leader or boss of the business. As you think about hiring personnel and organizing your workforce, you must also confront your desire and ability to be a good boss. Decide how you will handle your employees' entitlements. For example, salaries and wages, their insurance and retirement benefits, as well as analyzing the extent of your knowledge of tax related issues.

STEPS TO WRITING THE BUSINESS PLAN

Organize all the relevant information about your business. Begin creating section headings and putting the appropriate information under the appropriate headings. Effectively separating your business' unique approach to each of these headings will organize your plan in a way investors find useful:

1. Title Page and Table of Contents
2. Executive Summary*, in which you summarize your vision for the company
3. General Company Description, in which you provide an overview of your company and the service it provides to its market

---

[97] "How to Write a Business Plan" was co-authored by wikiHow Staff. 29 March 2019. https://www.wikihow.com/Write-a-Business-Plan. CC-BY-NC-SA.

4. Products and Services, in which you describe, in detail, your unique product or service
5. Marketing Plan, in which you describe how you'll bring your product to its consumers
6. Operational Plan, in which you describe how the business will be operated on a day-to-day basis
7. Management and Organization, in which you describe the structure of your organization and the philosophy that governs it
8. Financial Plan, in which you illustrate your working model for finances and your need from investors

*The executive summary should be less about the nitty-gritty details of operations and more about your grand vision for the company and where it is headed.

WANT.AN.EXAMPLE?
WANT.A.SAMPLE?

EXAMPLE: "KITCHEN GRABS."

EXECUTIVE SUMMARY
The need for fast, easy, fuss-free and delicious meals continue. Kitchen Grabs is a healthy alternative to fast meals.

PRODUCT AND SERVICE
Kitchen Grabs are pre-packed meals prepared daily made available in restaurants and online. The meal selection will vary per day designed by a dedicated nutritionist working with our passionate cooks to ensure that each meal approximates the dietary nutritional requirements of the average adult.

The meal selection will be made available online only on the previous day. Fresh ingredients go into each delectable dish. Upon posting, customers can pre-order for meals to be consumed the following day.

Kitchen Grabs' restaurant, a chic and homey diner-style setup, charmingly sits on the corner of Delaney Ave. and 2nd East St., nestled in the ever-active business district of Houston. Walk-ins are welcome. Residents and workers from the surrounding buildings can order online (www.kitchengrabs.com) or through phone (4-KGRABS or 454-7227) and their meals will be delivered hot and surely delicious.

MARKET ANALYSIS
Business advisers say that the food industry is saturated, and any new entrant faces huge obstacles. For us at Kitchen Grabs, these obstacles are giants – the established fast food chains and the vending machines. Yet we cower not. We sincerely believe in our meals. Further, we strongly believe that healthy and delicious meals will never run out of patrons. In fact, customer satisfaction concerns us way more.

Our target market are adults, male and female, from 16 years old and above, residing and/or working within a radius of 8 blocks from the restaurant. They are generally subject to rigorous activities (physical and mental) and need sustenance to properly perform their tasks. Their activities take up most of their waking hours, more like, working hours. A quick meal will always be a welcome help.

SALES AND MARKETING STRATEGY
Prior to the setup of the restaurant, Kitchen Grabs was an online cafeteria. We initially served the hungry workers of several companies in Houston's business district and they wanted more. Whenever we participated in trade fairs, the top question was whether we have a 'real' store; a funny question but an incessant one eventually urging us to construct our first restaurant. We will continue to attend bazaars and trade fairs spreading the word on health and available options, particularly our meals. For the next year, we intend to harness social media further.

OPERATIONS AND MANAGEMENT
The company was founded by a brother and sister tandem, Neil and Collette Viola. She studied nutrition while he trained yuppie clients. His random advice requests turned into serious discussions on health, fitness, and the inconvenience of healthy options. These became the foundation of Kitchen Grabs. Four years later, the Viola siblings still discuss how to make choosing health easier, though this time with more minds involved. Part of the team now is Dr. Linda McKann a health and nutrition consultant, George Willis with sales and operations, and Millie Dawson in finance. There is also Mama Edna Viola for taste and overall quality testing.

FINANCE
Two years into operations, Kitchen Grabs has broken even. However, as expansion was necessitated particularly the construction of the restaurant, the company secured bank loans to augment revenue. As business continues to grow, the company will be needing additional delivery riders and equipment for better service in the amount of $25,000. Appendix A computes the return of investment given the projections. Business projections predict a larger demand, an exciting new chapter for the owners and staff alike.

POSSIBLE ASSIGNMENT:
Create Appendix A, mentioned above in the last paragraph.

COMMENTARY

A commentary[98] is similar to a **review** in that it verbally or textually criticizes something. In this case, commentaries might criticize: a piece of writing, a data set, or a situation.

LITERARY COMMENTARY

Yes, whether you're a teacher, editor, student, or amateur critic, knowing how to constructively analyze someone's work is a useful skill. There isn't a magical formula for writing a commentary. The commentary you write depends upon what you're reviewing, why you're giving feedback, and what you think about the work. No matter what you're working on, having a clear goal and strong writing will help make your commentary successful.

When composing a literary commentary, use specific examples to support your thesis. State an issue or theme you've identified, show where you've found it in the work, then explain what effect the issue or theme has on the work.

Lastly, make sure to connect your examples back to the theme. When you use specific examples, make sure that you clearly illustrate how it connects back to the larger theme.

DATA COMMENTARY

A data commentary[99] is similar to other types of commentaries in that it requires you to analyze an existing set of information. But instead of commenting on a book, you are analyzing set of data.

One of the key components of a data commentary is synopsis of the research. You need to concisely write about the results of the study and why it is important. Make sure to analyze and summarize the data. For example, if the research is about the graduation rate in the Chicago Public Schools, you need to explain the numbers and illustrate why the results are important.

In a data commentary, you will likely want to use charts or graphs to help illustrate the results. You will then want to comment on and analyze those visuals.

SOCIAL COMMENTARY

When we use anecdotal evidence to hypothesize our lives (ex: "If I was a male teacher, my students would treat me better"), we are verbally giving a social commentary on the situations around us. Sometimes, commentaries like this don't provide scholarly evidence which makes them less serious and less "academic," but they still provide worthy trains of thought.

---

[98] "How to Write a Commentary." Co-authored by Alexander Peterman, MA, Education. Updated: April 23, 2019 https://www.wikihow.com/Write-a-Commentary. Under an CC-BY-NC-SA License, wikiHow's text content is free to modify, republish and share.
[99] "How to Write a Commentary." Co-authored by Alexander Peterman, MA, Education. Updated: April 23, 2019 https://www.wikihow.com/Write-a-Commentary. Under an CC-BY-NC-SA License, wikiHow's text content is free to modify, republish and share.

EXAMPLE: ME AS A FUTURE PARENT BY MAKAI B.[100]

Life is never easy. But our parents make it seem as easy. And that's why most of us look up to them because they make a big impact on her life. So when you grow up are you gonna be like your parent? I'll tell you what I think about this question.

Growing up we are told to look up to our parents. They are role models so the question was asked " Will I become one of my parents in the future?" and I answered yes. The reason why I will turn it to one of my parents because my parents are kind of loving people. They are always wanted your time to volunteer their time. They're always there to listen to you. My parent's career is different from mine because I'm going to the medical field. Where my dad does odds and ends jobs, Whereas my mom does have a degree in nursing so I guess it's kind of the same. I will raise my family differently because I want to go on more family trips whereas my family didn't due to personal issues. In psychology, children develop learned behavior and it starts from childhood so I believe I will follow the same path but a little bit more curves, but not so many detours

In conclusion, Most people don't want to end up following their parents and some do, but I believe every individual has their own path. It doesn't matter how you were raised it only matters how you finish your life and are you proud of what you doing. Parents are there to set us an example of what life is capable of. No matter the bends or the detours. What matters is family and if you stayed together you can go through anything.

---

[100] Thank you Makai, a student from the Spring 2020 semester. Their piece is licensed CC-BY-NC-SA.

EMAIL

Email[101] is the remediated version of the letter. We're still supposed to use a greeting and a closing; we're supposed to be brief, and, yes, there are "return addresses" involved, just as there are attachments like there used to be enclosures.

Email is the new letter. I'm repeating that because it's not the new or old text message. It's not Snapchat. It's not Facebook. It's still supposed to be – especially if the intended audience is a teacher or boss – a "professional" form of communication.

So, basically, some of the same principles that we learn about writing letters can be used when learning about how to write an email message. Think for a few seconds about your audience. Then think for a few more seconds. Make sure to capitalize the person's name, use correct punctuation, and spell words correctly. Adding a closing is a bonus!

A DEEPER DIVE

Historically, email was an informal way of communicating to other workers. Email straddles the line between informal communication and formal business interaction. Communicating via email can be difficult to deal with in a business setting because of the inability to tell emotion or tone of typed text. Caution must be used when writing emails in a professional business setting.

Keep in mind the following tips when composing an email.
- Limit email use in the workplace to business-specific information and topics.
- Review email for legal implications, because any and all written documents in a business environment can be used in court.
- Use professional language and tone.
- Pay attention to your audience and consider their background when writing.

AUDIENCE: INTENDED VS. UNINTENDED

Every document that is created is normally crafted to someone specifically. This someone would be your intended audience, for your writing style, and content will be tailored to their appeal. Email messages, unlike some other business documents, are not restricted to just one person, or intended audience.

All aspects of your business documents should take into consideration everyone that could potentially read it. By ensuring this, you will save yourself and even possibly save your job.

As mentioned above, you never know who will be reading your documentation, so if an unintended reader who is not authorized to read or use your document, decides to use it, they could be putting themselves and others in significant danger.

---

[101] "Professional and Technical Writing/Business Communications/E-Mail." *Wikibooks, The Free Textbook Project.* 22 May 2016, 20:17 UTC. 25 May 2016, 18:49 <https://en.wikibooks.org/w/index.php?title=ProfessionalandTechnicalWriting/BusinessCommunications/E-Mail&oldid=3084147>.

PROFESSIONAL EMAIL MESSAGE BY LIZ[102]

Dear Dr. Richman:

My name is Liz, and I am a current student at the Wahpeton NDSCS campus who is taking part in the culinary arts program. Since I have been attending for almost a full year now, I would like to provide some feedback on the school.

One benefit is that there is a lot of activies avaliable for students to do outside of classtime. Because of that, it is easier to feel more relaxed and enjoy campus life. Another benefit is that the instructors are well trained, so students can trust them to have knowledge about the field that they are teaching. The one major pitfall that I have noticed is that the technology that we use is not totally up to date and/or the instructors are not fully sure how to use it, but I understand that there is only so much that can be done about it.

In conclusion, I would just like to say that despite the school not being perfect, there is no perfect school either, so I enjoy campus life and classes here at NDSCS for the most part.

Sincerely,
Liz S

QUESTIONS:

- o How do you know when you've written an effective email?
- o What is the difference between a "bad" email and a "good" email? Or is it too subjective to define?

---

[102] This lovely email was created during the Spring of 2021. Please note that even though Liz brought up a pitfall of the college, she kept her "professional tone" in tact. This piece is licensed CC-BY-NC-SA.

Maya
@themayannn

I seldom apologize in emails.

Alternatives:
- Thanks for flagging!
- Good catch - I will make the updates/changes.
- Many thanks for noticing the error, [name], we will [verb]
- Thank you for bringing this to our attention. We will [verb]

Stop over-apologizing at work.

9/11/18, 11:21 AM

3,486 Retweets **9,142** Likes

ESSAY

"Essays[103] are brief, nonfiction compositions that describe, clarify, argue, or analyze a subject. Students might encounter essay assignments in any school subject and at any level of school, from a personal experience 'vacation' essay in middle school to a complex analysis of a scientific process in graduate school."

I've written essays about all sorts of topics. I've written an essay about whether shaved heads on women are attractive, I've written an essay about Chuck Klosterman being a god and theoretically having his own religion (serious, it's even in a BOOK), and I've written essays about everything in between.

The range of topics for the genre of ESSAY is varied beyond belief. Just as the topics for any given essay in any given writing class are varied, so are the lengths, the audiences, and the formats. You might have one instructor who tells you that the five-paragraph essay is the bomb.com and then the next instructor will say, "Be creative! Ditch that five-paragraph crap!"

WANT.AN.EXAMPLE?
WANT.A.SAMPLE?

EXAMPLE: "LAS ESPINAS DE MI ROSA" BY M[104]

Imagine growing up in the United States, being exposed to many ethnic groups and cultures, coming together and getting along with no issue or problem at all. Wouldn't that be amazing? If ALL races from many cultures came together and rose above with one another? Well here in this lovely country of The United States of America – shit like that does not fly by that easily. This is a snapshot of my story of being born on this soil of hatred, racism, sexism, in a misogynistic country. I hope to share this piece with you, the reader, the audience, whomever you are – please read and inhale what I am gifting to you. Writing this piece was an intense moment for me. My former professor at Minneapolis College asked me to write a piece about my run-ins with racism and hatred from others when I shared one of my stories from my past in class one time. It took a lot of courage and strength to write this, but I do hope this does give you an eye opener that racism is real and has been alive for centuries. I hope one day we do change this and put it to death and move on from it. No good comes from evil.

The first time that I am speaking of is my first encounter with racism. This is something I did not even know existed or heard of. This was something that did scar me for a very long, long time and my innocence was taken from me. Let me break it

---

[103] Fleming, Grace. "What an Essay Is and How to Write One." ThoughtCo, Sep. 18, 2019, thoughtco.com/what-is-an-essay-p2-1856929.
[104] Las Espinas de mi Rosa by M. is licensed under a Creative Commons Attribution- NonCommercial-NoDerivs 4.0 International license. https://creativecommons.org/ licenses/by-nc-nd/4.0/legalcode

down for you what happened, this may shock and "wow" so just be aware. I was at a park, happily playing on the playground area and sliding the down slide over and over again, swinging back and forth as the air pushed me, each sway and a sun kiss each time I swayed forward. Just being a kid – with no worries or negative thoughts in the world *but something dark always interrupts the fairytale. This, the first time.*

I was playing on the playground and this girl that was my age approached me and asked if I wanted to play with her. I said yes because I was told to be nice and kind to those who are nice and kind toward me. I remember what she looked like and what she was wearing but her name is a blur to me. She was blonde, blue eyes like the water. I swear if you stared too long you might drown in them, pale and fair skin with a pink shirt and yellow and polka dotted shorts. She was cute and a fearless young girl. We played and played, laughing out loud like this could be the best day ever, but it turned for the worse. Her grandfather was an older man with blonde and white hair, pasty and burnt skin color, and blue eyes like the little girl's but his eyes had red veins in them. Like he hadn't slept for days and days or was mad as Hell at someone. He was mad-- at *me.* He told his granddaughter "they" had to go because it was getting dangerous. She looked around and pulled back from him. I was looking around because I got uncomfortable with what was going on. It was sad seeing this girl dropping her face, and her smile disappearing. I was focusing on her and did not realize her grandfather pushed me away from her and called me names and spat on me.

I was numb. The girl began to cry and pushed her grandfather, which woke him up, realizing how badly he fucked up. I turned around and went to my Dad with spit and sadness drenched into my pores and soul. My father looked at me and wiped the spit off me and asked what happened and who was responsible. I kept my head down and did not want to talk but I found it in me to point at the old man. My father walked toward his direction. I remember my brothers running toward them. You could hear them arguing and yelling at each other. Next thing, my father pushed the old man over the playground and had his fist up but saw me looking at him and walked away. The little girl was crying and crying, and nothing made it right. The old man started to feel guilty and ashamed as the bystanders shook their heads at him and he looked at his granddaughter. That was the first time and day racism made its presence in my life. This is something that made me scared to talk to any other race other than my own but even my race was mean to me.

I lost faith in humankind at a young age and that should have not been the case. Kids learn from us. Kids can see what is going on and comprehend a little bit. Just a little bit could hurt that child for long time – like it did me and many others who experienced this act a young age. Many of you are wondering what happened afterwards. Well, we did not call the police, and the police did not show up. We simply left and did not go out for many weeks to parks, lakes, or malls. We simply avoided any area that White people were in. I would not talk to one or even look at them in the eye. I had a fear of them. I was scared to approach any kids or adults that were White. I struggled a lot in school, but I tried my hardest to not show it at home. My father felt powerless after the event. He started to withdraw from everyone that was not family or close friends. He simply did not like to talk to anyone unless he had to.

My father told me a story about when he first to the United States in the '80s, and that was it was different. People were calmer, nicer, more welcoming, and simply did not mistreat you by the color of your skin. It just did not happen at all.

I had a hard time believing it because of my experience with it. He stated that during the Reagan Administration, he felt welcomed here. He was excited to come here and get all the opportunities that he could and provide for himself and his family back home. My father's story was very similar to my mothers' as well. She too came here during that era. They stated they never faced racism at all until my experience. I felt like there was some root of evil that was birthed hundreds of years ago but is now making its appearance again in this era. But it starts with one man, our "amazing leader" – Mr. Number 45 himself. I refuse to mention his name. It disgusts me to my very core.

When the 2016 Presidential Elections happened, it was saddening and shocking to see all the hatred, bigotry, homophobia, and racism be birthed again. It was sad to see where America was heading. We were going to a dead end – fast. Watching all the ridiculous and irrational candidates on both sides was funny and sad at the same time. I could not believe that these individuals could have a job that gave them power. The rest of the individuals were just as foolish as he was. 45's facial expressions would get to me. I wonder how his family could stand the sight of him. I wonder how anyone can? I always questioned what was so great about this man? There was nothing amazing about him at all. He did not seem like he was a man that could lead a company because he was bankrupt. But how did we let him be in charge of our country? I was devastated with the outcome of the elections.

When this man was running, all presentations at each state were heart wrenching to watch. I could not believe that people were there to support him! I was sad to see children and women there. This man nationally and internationally said, "GRAB THEM BY THE PUSSY." Like who the fuck says that shit? That is so nasty and not what a president would say. It's not their demeanor. This man has children of his own – daughters. What would make it okay for someone that is going to lead a nation to be taken seriously like that? What would make it okay for a nation to think this is funny and stand behind him? What would make it okay for someone to say bigoted and racist things where the minority population is growing? HOW? Can someone please to explain to us?

This man called Hispanics "criminals, rapists, and thugs" and said Middle-Eastern people should be banned. Everything was being reversed that the Obama administration was trying to do or get done. We are being oppressed and challenged under this administration. I felt targeted even though I am from here. I was being asked by people if I was born from here or if I had DACA because I am a minority. I was disgusted with both genders belittling me because I was shade darker than them. I was tired of being called names or of having people ask me if I enlisted to become documented; it pissed me the fuck off. I was scared to go out because of the possibility of encountering one of these mad people. I did not even want to speak my foreign language because I did not want to be targeted anymore; I was scared to take my child with me. I was sad that she came in the era where racism comes in all ages and shades. I was scared of it. I did not want her to be exposed to it while being out in public with me. I mean who would? Who would want to have kids in this time? It is not a time to be alive. It is not a time where progress is being made. It is not. I never felt so ashamed to be in the skin color that I am until I came to this college. I always felt so targeted before I came here. This school was a safe haven for me. Like it probably was for many others. I love everything about being a minority. Being Latina. I am a rose in the making and will establish my roots deep in this world. For those of my own to carry it on.

45 will never silence me. He pushes me to be the hardest, strongest, and ambitious Latina. I promised my daughter that I will not let this man stereotype us and oppress us. I will rise above it all. The stereotypes, the statistics, and those who are believing that we are just "greasers that take everyone's jobs," – that was something that I could not stand hearing because no one was taking anyone's job. My people would work the shit jobs that require hard work and long days. I remember my parents working these jobs before they got better jobs that they have now. When you go on the streets of the Twin Cities and the surrounding suburbs of these cities, you see **mainly** Caucasian men or women on these streets begging for money instead of a job. This is a fact that we never address at all, but we can acknowledge Hispanics coming into this country "stealing jobs and doing crime" here on the news, or wherever else. I never felt we were stealing jobs or doing crime – *some of us do but not all of us do.* Therefore, I feel we should not be stereotyped by these stigmas at all. It is rude and arrogant to do.

I always worked hard since I was sixteen-years-old because I got tired of depending on my hard-working parents, and I wanted to see what it was like to work and go make my own money. When I was a junior in high school, you think of the future a lot because there's pressure in America to know what you want to do with yourself by the start and end of your senior year. At the beginning of senior year, there was a staff waiting at this board where all seniors are supposed to go and write down where they were going after high school. I did not have anything until I was the last to put on there that I was going to the military. Oh yes, I went off to the military – how chaotic and insane of me, right? I legit thought that I was going to be a badass and saving this country from our "enemies" overseas but in reality, our enemies are on this land of ours. Do not get me wrong, it was an amazing experience because I learned about myself a lot and made a new family but there were some low and ugly parts of this world that I wish did not exist.

Let me fast forward you to the day that I met my new leader; he was pretty cool at first and seemed like he was going to care for me but as the years went on and on, he became more of a prick. An asshole. Of course, you cannot say a thing to your superiors because you are *"supposed"* to show respect to them, however, I do think you should give respect when it is earned. I mean isn't that how things should be? But as the 2016 Presidential Elections came around, I did see a whole new side to this individual that I did not like at all. I started to not like going there; I felt uncomfortable there. The family that I did make had a different side to them that I thought would never exist. I did not like this reality of these people as they would state their opinions of 45's speeches and how they *did* agree with him. I started to hear "I am not trying to offend you but......" That saying would irk and make my blood boil quickly. Hearing that did make me change my ways and views on those that would say and make excuses about 45's speeches, talks, and policies. Trust me--- seeing and hearing the way these people would talk about him like he was some God was disturbing. *"He really cares about the people."* Oh yeah? What people? Here is the best one yet, *"he is going to take care of the military and refund us a lot of money. He is going to give us a raise and better bonuses."* I know what you are feeling, you just want to say "wow" or just want to laugh. Trust me, I laughed so hard in these people's faces. This was the nature that I was exposed to after this man was running for president and became president. I don't even acknowledge him as the president because that is something that he is *far* away from. A president is supposed to be a leader, a rational person, and someone who cares for those that help and build more opportunities in their homeland. The lovely individual that we are stuck with, is not; this man is filled with animosity, hatred, racism, and bigotry.

If I could go back and not enlist, I probably would if I knew what the future was going to hold. I wanted to go all out and prove to those that I could become someone, and that, I still am doing. Do not get me wrong. I did meet some amazing individuals along this process, and it did teach me a lot about myself in this journey.

Another path of this journey of being exposed to racism happened recently at Target. Imagine joking and laughing in Spanish and turning to hear someone say, "why can't people learn the language here.?" Yes, that did happen to me. I still remember the old hag that said that to me. I was pretty disgusted and ashamed of the human race. I tell ya, I wanted to punch life and soul out of that waste of a life human being. A mother who had 3 kids with her watching this. They looked embarrassed and ashamed that their own birth giver said those wrenching words as they knew their mother fucked up at that moment right there. My mother, she is pretty old school and does not take shit from ANYONE. She was enraged and went to the lady and yelled at her where another elder woman, who witnessed this, stepped in and defended my mother. The woman told her she should be ashamed in herself as she is teaching her children how to hate and that is not good. The elder woman did handle this case pretty classy you should say. I would have never thought to hear someone step in and show someone their true ugly colors. As the older woman was defending my mother, the offender's husband came around the corner. He was confused and asked why his wife was being attacked. The older woman scolded him about his wife and the man looked embarrassed and grabbed the kids and left the store. Others looked at her in disgust as she just stood there in shame. The store manager came around the corner and asked her to leave. The lady asked and pleaded to finish her shopping and that she would not bother others; the manager refused and proceeded to tell her to leave and that they did not accept that type of behavior. The lady started to cry, stated that she was sorry, and left as we shook our heads at her. We hugged the old lady and thanked her for helping us out.

I felt so powerless in that moment. That my daughter was there to witness this animosity. I was pretty silent and quiet after that event. I was very serious. I did little communication with my mother afterwards. My mother knew I was so upset and did not want to talk. I had no intentions anyway. I had no reason why I needed to speak anymore. I was scared to be scorned by another person for embracing my first language by using it. I feel like I'm seeing this happen everywhere else. Others feel as scared as I do to embrace who I am. Where I come from, I am not 100% American to the White culture. I wonder to myself, what is an American? Because when you think of it, America belongs to the Natives and Mexicans before the colonizers took it from them.

This is just a piece of my story to you. I hope you take these small stories and learn from them. Learn to love your neighbor and appreciate them for who they are. This does go a long way as well. Being evil and filled with hatred does not benefit you in the long run. I learned a lot in these obstacles that I came across and overcame. I became very resilient and open to those around me. Whether you are Black, Asian, White, etc. I appreciate you all and I hope you learn to spread love and good from one and another. I hope one day all groups will be able to reunite and become as one and will rise together.

+

Mikey
@__MikeyMartin

History essays in 2053: "Explain the use and role of memes as a coping mechanism during the Corona Virus Pandemic of 2020"

105

---

[105] Tweeted April 2, 2020. There are MANY tweets with this message out there, by the way. I suppose one could argue there's a lot of plagiarism on the Twitter?

HOW-TO GUIDE

How-To Guides can be found anywhere, but we typically receive them with packaging. Sometimes they are well-written, and the reader doesn't question how to attach THING A TO THING Z. But if they are off in their wording, or the pictures aren't clear, we end up in frustration with an item that doesn't function.

What are the parts of a well-done How-To Guide?

- Introduction
- Materials Needed
- Steps

For a document[106] to be efficient in this way, it must be easily understood by the intended audience. It is important to use simple sentences, words, and structure so that all that view the document can comprehend it. A document that is hard to understand is not usable or effective, since the audience will be unable to properly understand the document. Highly usable writing should help readers quickly locate, understand, and use the information to complete their task(s).

WANT.AN.EXAMPLE?
WANT.A.SAMPLE?

HOW TO BE A NERD[107]

INTRO:
Whether you are already a nerd or want to embrace your inner nerd more, these instructions will aid you in either quest to up your nerd game or at least jumpstart it.

MATERIALS NEEDED:
- Fake glasses with thick rims, if you don't already wear glasses or wear contacts
- A lot of books about philosophy or history or language, so stick with nonfiction
- Solitude
- A collection of music, on vinyl or digital, that no one has ever heard of

STEPS:
1. Wear fake glasses, if you don't already wear "real" ones.
   a. If you actually have to wear contacts or glasses already, you should dispose of them and only wear fake ones. Buy many different kinds, but remember that the bigger they are, the better. And the blacker, the better as well – red frames are fairly geeky, but black says, "I'm serious about

---

[106] "Professional and Technical Writing/Rhetoric." Wikibooks, The Free Textbook Project. 6 Apr 2012, 12:26 UTC. 24 Feb 2021, 21:45 <https://en.wikibooks.org/w/index.php?title=Professional_and_Technical_Writing/Rhetoric&oldid=2302407>.
[107] Example created by Sybil Priebe, licensed CC-BY-NC-SA.

these fake frames, now leave me alone so I can do my calculus homework."

2. Start reading up on as much factual information as possible.
   a. Bonus for connecting philosophy and history and language.
   b. Double bonus if you bite on your fake glasses while looking off into space when thinking really hard about what you just read.
3. Start writing or blogging about what you are reading.
   a. Bonus for using Twitter or Reddit to pontificate.
4. Read the dictionary more often than you used to so you truly understand words like "pontificate."
5. Begin to worry less about hygiene and appearance.
   a. Doing any sort of hair maintenance is forbidden, but one should consider messing it up when they are talking to people. That's how Einstein's got that fuzzy & frizzy white-puff-ball-look; only nerds know that.
6. Eat for those brain cells.
   a. Your brain survives off of carbs. This is fact. So, to nourish the body is to nourish the intellectual inside of you.
7. Live mostly in solitude and be a secretive hermit.
   a. When in class, whether you're writing a note or texting or taking a test, make sure to hunch over like it's a secret code you are jotting down. Secretive people, the "quiet ones," are the ones people point to as total nerds.

LETTER

Paper means more than an email. It takes extra time to write up a letter and mail the sucker off. Businesses are aware of this.

When my sister was in high school and trying to get her first job, she interviewed at a local grocery store. She interviewed horribly because it was her first time, so after telling this story at a family gathering, our uncle suggested that she send a Thank You letter. She did. She explained her nervousness, she thanked him for the experience, and… yes, she got a call back! They offered her a part-time gig!

Letters vary in motivation and in their messages. Some letters are written without the need for a response, some are written with a simple message of "Hi," and some letters are harsh like complaint letters to companies and are meant to be that way.

THE DIFFERENCE BETWEEN LETTERS[108]

The main thing that differentiates a business letter from other letters is that a business letter is a legal document. The writer can be held liable for anything written in the letter. For example, if it is stated that a project will be completed by a certain date in a business letter, the project legally must be completed by that date. However, if the project can't be completed by that date, another letter can be written stating that the project is behind schedule and why. For this reason, business letters must be written differently than letters used for personal use.

A business letter is used primarily to request or provide information, to relate a deal, to bring or continue conversation, and/or to discuss prior negotiations. A business letter can be classified as private; however, it is typically not circulated to others, but rather meant for the eyes of the participants involved. Therefore, a business letter needs to be clear, focused, and to the point. When writing a business letter, the author should avoid interjecting personal stories.

FORMATTING YOUR LETTERS
- Use single spacing. There is no need to double space a business letter.
- Use a simple format with font that is easy to read.
- Leave a blank line between each paragraph. This makes it easier to follow the changes of topics within the letter.

TIPS ON WRITING LETTERS
- Address the letter to a specific person whenever possible, and not the company in general so it does not get discarded.
- Use company letterhead to make the document more professional if the document is related to company affairs.

---

[108] "Professional and Technical Writing/Business Communications/Letters." *Wikibooks, The Free Textbook Project.* 26 Mar 2016, 21:00 UTC. 11 May 2016, 18:31
<https://en.wikibooks.org/w/index.php?title=ProfessionalandTechnicalWriting/BusinessCommunications/Letters&oldid=3066458>.

- Collect all the information you will need for your letter and jot down the basic order in which you plan to cover this information. Organize your material in the most persuasive order.

WANT.AN.EXAMPLE?
WANT.A.SAMPLE?

EXAMPLE: COMPLIMENTARY LETTER TO A COMPANY

Andrew Thomas
**** *th Ave N
Wahpeton, ND 58075

February 09, 2021

Timberland Boots & Clothing
200 Domain Dr
Stratham, NH 03885

Dear Timberland,

I've been a customer of yours for quite a few years. Mostly just your boots for work, but a few other thaings as well. I'm writing to give you my feedback about my expiriences with your products..

I have not had an easy job since I was aproximately sixteen. Be it construction or factory work its always been very physical for me. I was also in the military so I like to think my feedback on boots holds a little weight. I have no complaints. In fact I only have words of praise for you. No matter how bad my job was your boots took the abuse and lasted for quite some time.

In closiing, you have an amazing product. You also have me as a lifetime customer.

Sincerely,
Andrew Thomas[109]

Alisa Priebe[110]
555 70th Avenue West, #555
Fargo, ND 58555

January 30, 2013

Human Resources
c/o Flint Communications
101 North 10th Street
Suite 300
Fargo, ND 58107

Dear Mr. Person:

I am writing to you to apply for the open position of Production Artist. I am an excellent candidate; I have strong communication skills, I'm a quick learner, and I have a fun, creative personality.

I earned a Bachelor of Arts degree in English from North Dakota State University. I chose this educational path because I am a strong communicator and I enjoy expressing myself. My writing abilities are exceptional; while my specialty is creative writing, I excel at technical writing as well. Not only did my education allow me to sharpen these skills, but my employment experience played a large part as well.

For example, at *Integreon*, a company which provides document support services to law firms and other corporations, I spent nearly three years corresponding with clients (mostly attorneys and legal secretaries) via email and telephone. Through these exchanges, I would follow a particular process: receive request to format, edit, or proofread a legal document; delegate the request to the appropriate coworker; review said request; and, return the request by the requestor's preferred timeline. I learned how to understand their needs and complete their requests accordingly.

While polishing my communication abilities, I was fortunate to become skilled at many different types of software. The training team at *Integreon* did an amazing job with its employees. Most training courses were required while others were available to expand your computer skills and complete a wider range of project requests. At every job since my time at *Integreon*, I have had fellow employees approach me and tell me that my computer and software skills are impressive. It is a true testament to both their training and my ability to learn quickly.

With many types of software, I have been able to create and design different documents. At *Warner and Company Insurance*, I created a recipe booklet of potluck favorites for the employees. At *Integreon*, I created the first team-specific newsletter

---

[110] This gem by the author's sister is licensed CC-BY-NC-SA.

115

which included images, quotes, short stories, and tips and tricks. At *Vogel Law Firm*, I acted as Co-Captain for the United Way drive and created certificates for prizes and "kudos" cards for employee appreciation.

In these experiences, I learned to communicate with clients to meet their needs, expand my computer knowledge and skills, and use my ability to create beautiful documents for many purposes. Please refer to my resume for further information. Thank you for your time and consideration. I look forward to hearing from you about how I can become an asset to your company.

Very truly yours,
Alisa Priebe

Dear Dr. Julie Jackson:

Thank you so much for the opportunity to sit down with you and Dr. Joseph Sanchez to discuss the Lab Assistantship at Harvard. I am grateful to be considered for the position. I think I will be an asset to your department, especially given my experience with dissecting frogs.

I was nice to chat with you about how much you adore the TV show *Big Brother*, and I really appreciate the natural lighting that you have all added to the employee lounge; I'm sure it will encourage people to hang out a while longer, thus increasing morale.

I look forward to hearing from you.

Sincerely,
Zelda Smith

LIST ESSAY

A list essay is just what it sounds like – an essay in the shape of a list. It's a detailed list with a focus, and sometimes list essays are humorous or sarcastic in nature. This genre typically mimics these two popular web sites = thoughtcatalog.com and mcsweeneys.com. On these sites, writers post essays, and sometimes those essays are in the form of hilarious/sarcastic lists.

WANT.AN.EXAMPLE?
WANT.A.SAMPLE?

"10 WAYS TO GET RID OF A DATE"[111]

1. Keep it wide open.

When you're on a date that you regret more than anything else in the world, you have to get rid of that person somehow. And no one wants to see the food on the plate in your big, wide open mouth falling out as you talk. This is the exact reason for doing it. Chew with full swing of the jaw, maybe even throw in a little cough or laugh so the food goes anywhere but your mouth.

2. Let the music take you away.

There is always going to be that one "OMG I LOVE THIS SONG" moment. Use it to your advantage. When one is trying to be all alone with just the two of you, get up and get moving! Swing those arms like you're a helicopter, jump up and down like you used to at those middle school dances, scream at the top of your lungs, "I LOVE THIS SONG!" Shake your head back and forth so your hair is all messy, even try break dancing, hey you never know how well that one might go for you. It's bound to make that date be so embarrassed that they wouldn't think twice about calling you again. If you really want to embarrass one, make sure you dance at a place that doesn't even have music, that's guaranteed to get a rise out of the person.

3. "So what's your take on zebras?"

Awkward conversations are never forgotten and will sometimes define the time you had. The more awkward it is the better chance you have of never seeing this person again. Bring up things like "so did you see me dog lick himself when you were waiting for me?" or when you have to go to the bathroom try "you might want to go wait somewhere else, it can get kind of loud in here…" When the waiter comes to take your order ask many, many questions. "What do you recommend, what do these five things have in them, are you allergic to anything?"

4. What to do with those hands…

Well, there's always a nose you can put your fingers in. That should embarrass your date enough, but if you want to take it farther there are a few other things to do. Complement your dates face and how nice and fresh it looks. Give it a nice big stretch and squeeze of the cheeks, maybe even a slap when you're done touching it all over. You can also scratch yourself. Scratch anywhere. On the legs, neck, face, arms, in the places where only you should scratch…that's something no one really wants to see that, but if it's going to work why not do it.

5. Have a staring contest.
Look right into those big, beautiful (or ugly) eyes and don't even think of looking away. When you're asked a question, just keep staring. Put on a creepy smile and pull the corners of your mouth all the way up to your ears. Your date won't know what to do with an awkward smile moment that never ends because there is no response coming with that smile.

6. Shrek always said "better out than it."
Don't try to be that polite person. If you have a burp, you better let it out. You never know what it's going to be like so just let it go. If the burp ends up being way louder than you thought it would be, then that's really good. But if it is, you better make sure you say "Did you hear that one!" If it's quiet you should probably let your date know that you can do way better than that and you'll have one to top that real soon.

7. Emotions get the best of us.
Whether you're a guy or a girl, everyone still cries. You might not have something to cry about but don't stop those tears from coming. While your eating, in the middle of a conversation just break down. Start bawling, over reacting, saying your ex's name (make one up if you don't have one), and making a scene. But this can only last for so long. Give the show about three minutes then you're a happy peach again.

8. Crushes.
Nobody wants to hear how anyone is better looking than them, whether it's a celebrity or someone you know. Talk about how cute or hot someone is and that you would "so much rather be with that person but you will have to do for now." Talk about how their smile isn't as nice, their teeth are a bit crooked, their skin is a bit too pale or too tan for your liking, how you don't really like anything at all about their personality. Pull up that picture you have on your phone and show him/her how good that person looks.

9. Pay more attention to your surroundings than your date.
When you're in a restaurant, you're obviously going to have other people sitting around you. Focus all your attention on the people next to you. Begin with talking to your date about what the people ordered. Tell him unhealthy it is for them and that they should order something better. Say that what they are wearing doesn't look good and that you could've picked something better out. Then just start talking to the people next to you and ignore your date all together.

MANIFESTO

A manifesto[112] is a document wherein a person, government, or organization outlines their intentions, motivations, and/or views. These texts ask and attempt to answer the question: What do I believe? The Declaration of Independence is a form of manifesto. There are artistic manifestos, philosophical manifestos, corporate manifestos, personal manifestos, and political manifestos. A religious manifesto is referred to as "a creed". The word manifesto comes from Latin, and it connotes something which is very clear and conspicuous. While the length and content of a manifesto varies between each one, any well-composed manifesto will not only present a clear attack on a worldview, but also a practical means to manifest goals. When writing a manifesto, you should keep all this in mind.

WRITING THE MANIFESTO

Identify yourself and your aims. This might include your personal beliefs, your worldview, and your experiences that directly inform your manifesto. By introducing yourself, your readers will have a better sense of your life course.
- Make sure that you share life details related to your ideas.
- Relate important experiences from work, school, or life that help readers see you as an authority.
- Mentioning your degree in art might be useful in an artist's manifesto, just as civil service would be worth mentioning in a political manifesto.

Include a thesis. There should be some unifying point to your manifesto. This is delivered in your introduction. It will be a compelling argument, connecting all your ideas together. Make sure you take time to craft a well-written thesis statement.

Explain your precepts in the introduction. A precept is an actionable ideal, an instruction meant to regulate behavior or thought. Tell your readers a little about what ideals they're going to read about, before they go into it. You don't want to say everything, just a little bit, so that readers can engage with your manifesto's larger picture. Give yourself at least one sentence to mention the main points of your manifesto.
- You can use bullet points to list your precepts.
- Follow a precept up with a sentence explanation if you need clarity but save most of your explaining for the body paragraphs. If it isn't merely presenting the precept, don't put it in the introduction.

Give a plan for action. Don't just provide your ideas. Offer a direction for change. Manifestos are revolutionary by nature. Though not all revolutions are equal in scale, all share in this desire for change.
- Focus on verbs to evoke a sense of action. Avoid verbs like "am/is/are", "have/has" and other passive constructions. For example: "Every artist manifests Art itself," instead of "Every artist is Art itself."

---

[112] This guide was co-authored by Megan Morgan, PhD; Updated: March 29, 2019. *Wikihow*. https://www.wikihow.com/Write-a-Manifesto

- Use concrete details. Avoid words like "thing" and "something", as these are not specific. For example: "Something in our political system disturbs me" becomes "Negligence in our political system disturbs me."
- Take a current problem and re-imagine it changed through your ideology.

FAQ

What's the key difference between a mission statement and a manifesto? A manifesto is a declaration of someone's intentions, motives or ideas. It usually proposes some changes that the group or individual thinks should be made to the current system of government. A mission statement is what a company sets itself as its intended goal.

WANT.AN.EXAMPLE?
WANT.A.SAMPLE?

EXCERPT FROM "I HAVE A DREAM" BY MARTIN LUTHER KING JR. [113]

I have a dream that my four little children will one day live in a nation where they will not be judged by the color of their skin but by the content of their character.

I have a *dream* today!

I have a dream that one day, down in Alabama, with its vicious racists, with its governor having his lips dripping with the words of "interposition" and "nullification" -- one day right there in Alabama little black boys and black girls will be able to join hands with little white boys and white girls as sisters and brothers.
I have a *dream* today!

I have a dream that one day every valley shall be exalted, and every hill and mountain shall be made low, the rough places will be made plain, and the crooked places will be made straight; "and the glory of the Lord shall be revealed and all flesh shall see it together."

This is our hope, and this is the faith that I go back to the South with.

With this faith, we will be able to hew out of the mountain of despair a stone of hope. With this faith, we will be able to transform the jangling discords of our nation into a beautiful symphony of brotherhood. With this faith, we will be able to work together, to pray together, to struggle together, to go to jail together, to stand up for freedom together, knowing that we will be free one day.

---

[113] For the full speech and its audio, go to this web site: https://www.americanrhetoric.com/speeches/mlkihaveadream.htm

And this will be the day -- this will be the day when all of God's children will be able to sing with new meaning:

My country 'tis of thee, sweet land of liberty, of thee I sing. Land where my fathers died, land of the Pilgrim's pride, From every mountainside, let freedom ring!

And if America is to be a great nation, this must become true.
And so, let freedom ring from the prodigious hilltops of New Hampshire.
Let freedom ring from the mighty mountains of New York.
Let freedom ring from the heightening Alleghenies of Pennsylvania.
Let freedom ring from the snow-capped Rockies of Colorado.
Let freedom ring from the curvaceous slopes of California.

But not only that:
Let freedom ring from Stone Mountain of Georgia.
Let freedom ring from Lookout Mountain of Tennessee.

Let freedom ring from every hill and molehill of Mississippi.

From every mountainside, let freedom ring.

And when this happens, and when we allow freedom ring, when we let it ring from every village and every hamlet, from every state and every city, we will be able to speed up that day when *all* of God's children, black men and white men, Jews and Gentiles, Protestants and Catholics, will be able to join hands and sing in the words of the old Negro spiritual:

Free at last! Free at last!

Thank God Almighty, we are free at last!

MEME

A meme[114] is any idea, behavior, style, or usage that spreads between people within a culture. In other words, a meme is a fad that carries cultural ideas, symbols, or practices and that spreads through writing, speech, gestures, rituals, or any other imitable phenomena. Internet memes are a subcategory of general memes. Any concept, catchphrase, or byword that spreads rapidly between users online can be considered an internet meme. This content tends to spread through internet-based communication platforms such as emailing, blogs, forums, image boards (e.g. Tumblr, Reddit, 4chan), social networking (e.g. Facebook, Twitter), instant messaging, and video-hosting services (e.g. Youtube, Vimeo). The sheer volume of users and speed of communication on the internet causes online memes to spread and evolve far more quickly than their offline counterparts, sometimes going in and out of popularity in only a matter of days.

[114] "Lentis/Internet Memes." *Wikibooks, The Free Textbook Project*. 30 May 2021, 08:57 UTC. 30 Nov 2021, 19:45 <https://en.wikibooks.org/w/index.php?title=Lentis/Internet_Memes&oldid=3839905>.

MEMO

Think of these like email messages on paper. In fact, email was pretty much remediated from paper memos and paper letters. Memos are general communication pieces that are in-house; a memo would go from a boss to another boss whereas a letter would go out-of-house from, let's say, a boss of one company to the boss of another or from an employee to a customer.

WANT.AN.EXAMPLE?
WANT.A.SAMPLE?

To: The Students of English 105
From: Sybil Priebe, Associate Professor
Date: October 18, 2011
Subject: Introduction of me.

BACKGROUND
It's relatively simple: I grew up in Wahpeton, went to NDSU for my bachelor's degree, taught high school in Minnesota, cruised back to NDSU for graduate school, and *BAM*, now I am here after lots of luck. I live in town after living in Fargo with my three younger siblings. They all live in Fargo.

FUTURE
Honestly, I'd like to stay at NDSCS and have the opportunity to teach different classes. Eventually, I'd like to have a lake cabin, a Saint Bernard & a Great Dane, and maybe I'll publish something really strange. In the immediate future, I plan to focus on fixing up the house we bought this summer.

HOBBIES
Obviously, I like teaching, and I consider it a hobby to do research on new ways to teach something. I also enjoy shopping, writing, and reading really odd literature. When I am not teaching or preparing to teach a class, I like to be running, walking, or biking = I did the Half Marathon this last May which was semi-torture.

LIKES
Walleye = ice-fishing
Volkswagens
Huge dogs

DISLIKES
Know-it-alls
Being sick
Chapped lips

THIS IS WHAT I REMEMBER

The memoir is a fairly straight-forward genre. It's what one remembers happening in his/her life up to a certain point.

> *Here's how I explain it to people who care to listen: if my siblings and I wrote about the last holiday we spent together, we wouldn't have the same stories. And no one would be wrong in their perspectives, unless they were just being silly.*

Memoir[115] is a specific type of narrative. It is autobiographical in nature, but it is not meant to be as comprehensive as biography (which tells the entire life story of a person). Instead, a memoir is usually only a specific "slice" of one's life. The time span within a memoir is thus frequently limited to a single memorable event or moment, though it can also be used to tell about a longer series of events that make up a particular period of one's life. It is narrative in structure, usually describing people and events that ultimately focuses on the emotional significance of the story to the one telling it. Generally, this emotional significance is the result of a resolution from the conflict within the story. Though a memoir is the retelling of a true account, it is not usually regarded as being completely true. After all, no one can faithfully recall every detail or bit of dialogue from an event that took place many years ago. Consequently, some creative license is granted by the reader to the memoirist recounting, say, a significant moment or events from his childhood some thirty years, or more, earlier. (However, the memoirist who assumes too much creative license without disclosing that fact is vulnerable to censure and public ridicule if his deception is found out, as what happened with James Frey and his memoir, *A Million Little Pieces*.)

Furthermore, names of people and places are often changed in a memoir to protect those who were either directly or indirectly involved in the lives and/or event(s) being described.

---

[115] "Basic Writing/Print version." Wikibooks, The Free Textbook Project. 9 Sep 2008, 16:02 UTC. 11 May 2016, 16:53 <https://en.wikibooks.org/w/index.php?title=BasicWriting/Printversion&oldid=1273791>. Licensed CC-BY-SA.

EXAMPLE: "FOLLOWING MY FATHER'S COURAGE" BY BETTY YANG[116]

Some of my friends describe the North side as the ghetto. Peers from college say it is extremely dangerous. I called it home for most of my life. The faint smell of grilling as I drove through the streets was a reminder that it was getting warmer out. In the summer, there were kids out throwing balls in the streets. Corner stores and gas stations were frequently busy. As a Hmong daughter, raised in a traditional home on the North side of Minneapolis, there were expectations of me since I was young. I had to learn the basics of cooking a meal, making sure there was rice, and doing well in school. I had to clean, do laundry, and help babysit as needed. It was an expectation for me to help my parents as much as I could. The decision to move in with my significant other was not an easy one as it took me a year to come to the conclusion. However, the more I did of what I wanted, the happier I felt.

Growing up, my dad had to learn how to hunt, how to farm, how to survive during a war, and how to provide for his family. He was reliable and smart. He was the oldest and the only son for most of his life. He has a younger sister and many years later, he has a half-sister and a half-brother.

When the war was ending and the American soldiers were leaving, Hmong people were completing forms and hoping to earn a spot to come to the U.S. It was a dark and gloomy day. The voices in the living area of the home became louder. My grandfather refused to go. "There are giants in the land you are moving to! You will get eaten if you move!" My dad made his decision to immigrate to the U.S. He is determined to live his life in a promising land, far away from the one he knew.

○

My dad would share stories about how poor he was as a child. He would tell us how far he had to walk just to go to school. It was so bizarre I almost don't believe it. He would have to wake up and prepare three hours ahead before his journey to school every morning.

In the dark, before the bright yellow sun rises, my dad would wake up at the crack of dawn. The loud "cock-a-doodle-doo" from outside meant it was time to start the day. There were no alarm clocks and the family's rooster was the only reliable alarm.

In the small corner of the house made of bamboo and hay, would be a small shadow of a young boy, turning pages of his one and only notebook he owned. My dad was always studious, trying as hard as he could to be ahead of his classmates. Although the rooster was the only other living creature up, there was no light to read or to study math by. My dad refused to be defeated by the lack of resources. It would have been easier for him to sleep in and wait until the sun rose for him to have light to study. Instead, my dad would gather sticks and logs of wood to start a little fire. He used the ashes from the fire as his light to study.

My father grew up with only one sister. She was about two or three years younger than him. While he was up studying, she was sleeping. While my father attended school, she stayed behind with my grandmother to farm and to feed the animals. They had three large plots of land to harvest fruits, vegetables, and rice.

When the sun started to rise and the temperature started to increase, it was time to start the long walk of five miles to school. Other children in the neighborhood followed one another to the same destination. The staggered group of young students traveled on the brown, dirt roads without any shoes, hoping they didn't step on anything that could cause infection.

There were days when he was late, and he would know what was coming once he gets to school – punishment. In front of his class, his teacher would make him kneel while holding a large rock in each hand. His hands had to remain at a 180-degree angle and if his arms fell below it, his teacher would use a long stick to hit the arm that was falling. The punishment was purposely done during class, as a way to publicly humiliate students who were late, who were caught cheating, or who misbehaved.

An hour later, he would wipe the dust off his black uniform pants and join his class. The day would go on as if he was never punished because students were frequently punished. Students were publicly disciplined so they would become more motivated to do better and to be more studious. There were not many options for the youth in the villages. They often had to pick between going to school or helping the family farm. Some youth did not have the luxury of picking and often times, those were young women. I think it is unfortunate that the girls, more frequently than not, automatically have to help the family babysit younger siblings and farm. The freedom to learn is sacrificed and I wish there were more opportunities for the young women to choose how they want to live.

I grew up very differently. My parents were more involved. I know I have more control of how I live my life. My mother and father did their best with what they had to raise the ten of us. Half of us shared the same father and the older half had their own. Their father died in the Vietnam War and a few years later, my mom married my dad. I have always viewed my older siblings the same as my other siblings. We all fought one another at some point and ganged up on each other at another. The rivalry was real. We built alliances and held grudges. We got even and this made my childhood complete.

The white truck with distinct music defined my childhood. The catchy loud song from a block away lets me know that the ice cream truck is getting close. Although my parents always warned us about buying ice cream from the ice cream man, my siblings and I would always beg my parents for some spare change just to be able to enjoy a small popsicle in the heat, on a sunny summer day.

On days when my parents didn't have money, my siblings and I would gather and hide inside the house and crack the windows wide open. When the ice cream truck rolled by, we would yell, "Stop!" as loud as we can. Once the truck stopped and we saw that no one was in line to buy ice cream, we giggled and lightly hit each other out of happiness that we got him. As soon as the truck started moving again, we would all yell, "Stop!" We did this until the truck passed our block. We had a ball.

As a child of ten, there wasn't always enough to go around. We all had our own hiding spots for popsicles in the freezer. It was survival of the fittest and we all made sure we'd make it.

When my parents came home from the grocery store, we all rushed outside to help bring groceries in. When it was time to divide the bag of candy, we all gathered at the table to make sure we each had a pile. The oldest at the table was responsible to evenly distribute the candy. Any leftover candy would end up in my parents' pile. Once we collected our pile, we all look for my dad to tell us where to hide our goods so that no one can get to them. One by one, we lined up to hear where my dad's secret spot was. When it was my turn, I leaned in and my dad whispered, "In your basket of clothes." It took me many years to figure out that we all had the same hiding spots, in our own basket of clothes.

○

At Washburn High School, I was taking some advanced classes and I was eager to figure out the next step in my life. The St. Olaf TRiO Educational Talent Search program did a tremendous job helping me apply to colleges. TRiO Educational Talent Search is a federally funded program that provides services to first generation, low-income and under-represented students. On the way home from the bus stop, I grabbed the mail and saw something for me. I knew right then that I had been accepted to St. Olaf College because of the thick white packet. I was ecstatic! Although I had many responsibilities at home, my parents always supported my academic endeavors. They knew my heart and they knew that I would come back with a degree.

In May 2014, I became the second person in my family of ten children to graduate with a Master's Degree. I earned a Master's in Non-Profit Management from Hamline University. At the time, I thought about running a program, because I believed in the outcomes. I have continuously set goals for myself with the support from my parents. I started seeing that my accomplishments were bigger than me. It was a chance for my parents to experience a glimpse of their dreams through me.

○

My dad was in his room, clicking away on his black Sony laptop. I sat down on the small stool and broke the news. I told my dad my decision. My dad didn't say much. He told me that when he made the decision to leave his father behind in Thailand to immigrate to the United States, his father and relatives felt neglected by him. My dad said, "Perhaps this is karma because I left my family."

"Dad? Today I'm moving out. It's not because I'm tired of living here with you and mom. I want to live on my own and I need to have my own space." I explained that I would still be around to help. I will come visit and buy groceries every now and then. As my dad was sitting down, I gave him a hug to reassure him that I will still be present in his life, even if I am no longer living with him under one roof.

After living with my family for five years after I graduated from college, I had decided to move out. Although I was nervous, I figured that it was time. I was in my late 20's, with two degrees, a car of my own, and a secure job. This is widely expected of adults in America. However, moving out before marriage is frowned upon in the Hmong community because I am a woman and I am not married.

I moved into a one-bedroom apartment in a suburb on the outskirts of the city. My roommate is my boyfriend. The quietness of the place brings both serenity and boredom. You can hear the clock tick when the TV is turned off. There is no one to fight over the remote. There are no more secret hiding spots in the fridge. I feel so thankful for my parents and the way they raised my siblings and me. I have always felt lucky to have such wonderful childhood memories. It contributed to my humility and it makes me want to do nice things for my parents as a way to thank them for raising us to be the best we can be.

Although some of his stories are not relatable, I have always admired my dad. I have had the privilege of living in a safe home with electricity and running water. I am thankful that my parents show that they care, and they support me. I rarely heard my dad complain about how hard life was. It was a way of living and it was what he only knew. His persistence and ambitions is what makes me want to be just as great as my dad. He is often the light that guides me when I am lost. My dad made decisions that will better his future, just like how I am making my own decisions to better mine as his daughter.

MULTI-GENRE

What happens when we COMBINE genres into ONE PROJECT?
It becomes its VERY OWN GENRE! So cool!
This chapter shows off one multi-genre project. There are so many possibilities to these sorts of projects; a multi-genre project could be personal or it could be about a research topic.

+

<u>Sybil's Definition</u>: This genre uses many genres to display research or to answer a question or to do just about anything; you could create the genres or find them. These genres can range from visual to technical: images, posters, reports, memos, email messages, Facebook posts, "To Do" Lists, notes, book snippets, articles, horoscopes, conversations, receipts, letters, ... basically anything that has text in it or communicates something to someone.

WANT.AN.EXAMPLE?
WANT.A.SAMPLE?

This example answers the question "Who am I?" with multiple genres.

I AM A TEACHER; I AM A CREATIVE PERSON.

To the People Who Care to Read this,

Maybe I should start with this: I have always liked school. I have always liked learning, sitting and taking in whatever knowledge my teachers could plop into my head, and I have loved creating. I live in my head - letting my thoughts grow into creative, crazy ideas. And as Steve Ward, one of my undergraduate professors, said: "It is in the process of creating where we learn the most. Not in the product."

> my whole being is a dark chant
> which will carry you
> perpetuating you
> to the dawn of eternal growths and blossomings
> in this chant i sighed you sighed
> in the chant
> i grafted you to the tree to the water to the fire.

My process, as he mentioned, began as a junior in high school. That is where my need, my desire, to compose started really. I had a small book I'd been writing, and maybe there is a distinct moment in English class where "it all started."

10 Nov 93

Trudy is telling me about her boyfriend AGAIN (sheesh) and sex… blahblahblah who knows. I'm trying to pay attention as geeky as that f##king is. Morris just said something about Henry David Thoreau and Ralph Waldo Emerson and transcendentalism. I am super curious. Who are these guys anyhow? What is this all about?

I would sit hunched over in class and highlight their words.

"What lies behind us and what lies before us are small matters compared to what lies within us." – Ralph Waldo Emerson

Oddly, at that time, I put my passion with words on the back burner. That same year, I took drafting technology classes at NDSCS and fell in love with the designs of floor plans. I urged my parents to allow me to go to North Dakota State University, but not because I wanted to be a writer - because I thought I wanted to be an architect. I thought I wanted to design houses, not sentences or lessons. I wanted to mimic my dad, with his career in construction.

life is perhaps
a long street through which a woman holding a basket
passes everyday
life is perhaps
a rope with which a man hangs himself from a branch

Then, during my freshmen year of college, depression hit once again just like it had my freshman year of high school. Suddenly, I questioned everything. I went on a bagel-a-day diet. I napped with a growling stomach and skipped classes.
But, slowly, I met people, fell for boy, and tried with all my might to reach out of a hole that I had jumped into.

life is perhaps a child returning from school.
life is perhaps lighting up a cigarette
in the narcotic repose between two love-makings
or the absent gaze of a passerby
who takes off his hat to another passerby
with meaningless smile and a good morning.

"They" say if you want to see change in yourself, fall in love. Love is insane that way, I guess. So, in Mason, I found parts of myself that I seemed to have lost after high school. My goofiness and my femininity.

Unfortunately, he gave me a false sense of security. I started to depend on him. My studies started to lack, and even though I changed my major to English Education, I still felt unsure about my future. My mother couldn't understand why I wanted to be a teacher rather than an architect, and Mason looked at my writings and wondered why I didn't sound more mature. The only people, at that time, that seemed to have faith in me and my abilities were me, my siblings, and my father.

life is perhaps that enclosed moment
when my gaze destroys itself in the pupil of your eyes.
and it is in the feeling
which i will put into the Moons impression
and the Nights perception
in a room as big as loneliness
my heart
which is as big as love
looks at the simple pretexts of it happiness
at the beautiful decay of flowers in the vase
at the sapling you planted in our garden
and the songs of canaries
which sing to the size of the window.
ah
this is my lot

Teaching was and is still my religion ("something one believes in and follows devotedly; a point or matter of ethics or conscience"). I told this to the people in Battle Lake, MN as they interviewed me a day in May of 1999, weeks after graduation. All I know is that they liked me enough to hire me on the spot.

my lot is
a sky which is taken away at the drop of a curtain
my lot is going down a flight of disused stairs
to regain something amid putrefaction and nostalgia
my lot is sad promenade in the garden of memories
and dying in the grief of a voice which tells me

I really, truly started to find myself in Battle Lake. Mason had ditched me, yet I found myself alone in a new world - in a relatively new job, with new students, and a new found freedom. Lots of soul-searching occurred that summer before I began teaching. Slowly, he left my mind, and peace entered. But being alone has always been easy for me. I could do the Walden thing.

"Many go fishing all their lives without knowing that it is not fish they are after."
– Henry David Thoreau

I could live alone on a lake without much contact with people and be OKAY. So, in my happy solitude, I threw my passions and energy into my teaching, into getting to know my students.

i love
your hands. i will plant my hands in the garden
i will grow i know i know i know
and swallows will lay eggs
in the hollows of my ink-stained hands.

131

I struggled. I went home at 4:30 most afternoons and would sleep until the next morning. My efforts seemed to be defeating me. And besides all that, my social life was lacking. The school wanted X; the students needed Y. My life yearned for Z. I kept trying to keep me above water.

> i shall wear
> a pair of twin cherries as earrings
> and i shall put dahlia petals on my fingernails

But I couldn't keep up the facade for long. I had to defend myself to many people yet wanted to teach with my liberal ways. Well, life doesn't work out that way – a person doesn't always get her way. Suddenly, in March, I got the letter from the superintendent asking me to meet with him and the principal. Female intuition kicked in. I was about to get canned.

In pure shock, I sat there as he told me that I, Sybil Priebe, someone who ALWAYS reached her goals, always had done everything RIGHT in her whole life, had, in fact, not added up to "district standards" as a teacher.

But I knew who I was, and I was not about to be defeated. So that same day, after writing an email to all my family and friends, I took out the Graduate School application that I had hidden in my desk. I filled out the missing parts, found some sample writings in my file cabinet, and used the postage from the school that was about to screw me over to mail it up to North Dakota State University. I would return to the campus that challenged me in the first place.

> there is an alley
> where the boys who were in love with me
> still loiter with the same unkempt hair
> thin necks and bony legs
> and think of the innocent smiles of a girl
> who was blown away by the wind one night.
> there is an alley
> which my heart stolen
> from the streets of my childhood.
> the journey of a form along the line of time
> inseminating the line of time with the form
> a form conscious of an image
> coming back from a feast in a mirror.

In graduate school, I found my path, my lot. I wanted to teach college freshmen – fresh meat – fresh minds. Others thought I should go on to get my Ph.D., but I knew that wasn't what was next. I also didn't think returning to my hometown was next for me, but it worked. And it worked well.

I am lucky enough to know that teaching and writing is where I want to be. I foresee many more struggles, but I am willing to not let them get me down. I will not let people make me question who I am. I know. And only I know.

and it is in this way
that someone dies
and someone lives on.
no fisherman shall ever find a pearl in a small brook
which empties into a pool.
i know a sad little fairy
who lives in an ocean
and ever so softly plays her heart into a magic flute
a sad little fairy
who dies with one kiss each night
and is reborn with one kiss each dawn.

Sincerely,
Sybil

Genres used: Letter, Poem, Journal Entry, Quotes, and a Definition

Works Cited

Emerson, Ralph Waldo. "Emerson: Quotes." *Transcendentalists.com*. Accessed 11 Apr 07. http://www.transcendentalists.com/emerson_quotes.htm

Farrokhazad, Forugh. "Another Birth." Poem. *ForughFarrokhazad.org*. Last updated 30 March 07. Accessed 11 Apr 07.
<http://www.forughfarrokhzad.org/selectedworks/selectedworks1.asp>

Priebe, Sybil. Journal Entry. 23 March 94.

"Religion." *Dictionary.com*. 13 Nov 07. http://dictionary.reference.com/browse/religion.

Thoreau, Henry David. "Thoreau: Quotes." Transcendentalists.com. Accessed 11 Apr 07. http://www.transcendentalists.com/thoreau_quotes.htm

Ward, Steve. Lecture. World Literature Class. North Dakota State University, Fargo, ND. 10 Dec 97.

OBITUARY

Losing a loved one[117] is a difficult process to go through but taking the time to write an obituary can help honor their life. An obituary can provide important information about your loved one, such as when they passed away and when the service takes place, but it can also paint a picture of the life they lived. After taking the time to write and revise your obituary, you can submit it to local papers so people know about how important your loved one was to you.

STEPS:

1. Announce the name and time of death in the first sentence. In your opening sentence, start with their name, where they lived, and when they passed away. You don't need to provide the cause of death if you don't want to. Keep the sentence brief and to the point so you can expand the obituary in other places.

2. Include a short summary of their life as the next paragraph. List the city where they were born, their parents, and important events that happened in your loved one's life. You can either list events chronologically or you can put them in order of what you feel is the most important. Try to use as few words as possible so the obituary is concise.

3. Add a short paragraph about hobbies, passions, or personal characteristics. Including personal details will capture the spirit of your loved one so others understand what their life was like. Create a list of hobbies or activities they actively participated in and how it affected other people.

4. List close family members in the third paragraph. Mention close family members, such as immediate family and parents, by name. When you want to list extended family, use a collective phrase or list the specific number. For others that have passed away before your loved one, use the phrase "preceded in death by," and use "survived by" before listing any relatives still living.

5. Provide details about the funeral service if it's public. If you're holding a public service, list the time and date along with the name of the funeral home. Make sure to list the specific details so others who were close to your loved one know where to go.

WANT.AN.EXAMPLE?
WANT.A.SAMPLE?

OBITUARY FOR EVERETT "SKIP" EARL EVANS[118]

Skip Evans passed away on December 20, 2020 at 43 years old.

---

[117] Jacobson, David I and Hunter Rising. "How to Write an Obituary." https://www.wikihow.com/Write-an-Obituary 15 Sept 21
[118] The author/editor of this textbook (Sybil) went to high school with Skip, and he was a good guy. She thinks he would be okay with his life being mentioned in this book, so students can learn about his life while practicing writing.

Skip was born on May 24, 1977 to Virginia and Everett Evans. He grew up in LaMoure, North Dakota attending elementary school and then moved to Wahpeton to attend middle and high school, graduating in 1995. During high school, he participated in many sports including football, basketball and baseball.

Skip attended North Dakota State University and earned a bachelor's degree in accounting. He briefly worked in accounting before pursuing his passion of flooring design and installation as an independent contractor. Skip loved spending time with his son, Bailey, especially attending Bailey's sporting activities and 'throwing the ball' around at Pelican Lake on holidays. He liked going to NDSU Bison football games with Bailey along with his family and friends.

Skip was an avid hunter and fisherman. He enjoyed spending time with his friends and attending sporting events of his nieces and nephews. Skip is survived by his son, Bailey Evans; nieces and nephews; and family and friends that loved him very much. Skip is preceded in death by his parents, Virginia and Everett Evans.

Interment will be at Fairview Memorial Gardens in Wahpeton, North Dakota at a later date. In lieu of flowers, memorials may be given to Youth Works at http://youthworksnd.org/. To send flowers or a memorial gift to the family of Everett "Skip" Earl Evans please visit our Sympathy Store.

POETRY

Poetry[119] is easy to recognize but hard to define.

Let's start with Webster's definition: "The art of rhythmical composition, written or spoken, for exciting pleasure by beautiful, imaginative, or elevated thoughts." As lovely as that sounds, it may already say too much about this unique and unpredictable art form. Rhythm is important; it's perhaps the only element in poetry we can truly count on. Rhymes are optional, but some sort of rhythm to the reading of quality poetry will always almost exist.

We can experience poetry through our eyes or our ears. It is usually meant to excite pleasure, but it can also reflect sorrow or regret. That brings us to "beautiful, imaginative, or elevated thoughts."

Writing poetry is fun. Find poems you love and share them with classmates/friends. Write love poems to your partner. Discover your own meanings in poetry and discuss those meanings without making them conform to an understood critical meaning. Poetry can be sweet or silly, short or long, fun, thoughtful, or personal. It can have more than one voice. Let poetry help you find connections in your life. Perhaps, you could use a poem as an intro to a science report![120]

POETRY DEVICES AND FORMS:

Poetry often uses particular forms and conventions to expand the literal meaning of the words, or to evoke emotional or sensual responses. Devices such as alliteration, onomatopoeia, and rhythm are sometimes used to achieve musical or incantatory effects. Poetry's use of personification, symbolism, irony, and other stylistic elements of poetic diction often leaves a poem open to multiple interpretations. To read more about poetic devices (which might also be called figurative language), head to the chapter on Figurative Language in this textbook.

DEVICES

ALLITERATION
Repetition of consonants, particularly at the beginning of words. Ex: It was the sweet song of silence.

METAPHOR
A direct comparison between two things. Ex: This classroom is as stale as a hospital.

IRONY
Occurs when something happens that is different from what was expected.

ONOMATOPOEIA
Words that imitate sounds like Bang! Or Meow!

---

119 "Choosing High Quality Children's Literature/Poetry." *Wikibooks, The Free Textbook Project.* 26 Feb 2013, 18:45 UTC. 18 Nov 2016, 16:47 <https://en.wikibooks.org/w/index.php?title=Choosing_High_Quality_Children's_Literature/Poetry&oldid=2492503>. Text is available under the Creative Commons Attribution-ShareAlike License.
120 This could easily be an assignment. Write a poem about your science report from a different class!

PERSONIFICATION
Giving humanistic characteristics to non-humans. Ex: The dog nodded in agreement.

SIMILE
A comparison using "like" or "as." Ex: That classroom is like a hospital.

FORMS

SONNET
A sonnet is made up of fourteen lines of rhymed iambic pentameter. Iambic pentameter is a line made up of five beats. English sonnets have a rhyme scheme of abab cdcd efef gg. It is usually one stanza long.

COUPLET
A pair of lines of verse. It usually consists of two lines that rhyme and have the same meter. Two words that rhyme can be called a couplet.

Example: I did but saw her passing by. But I shall love her till I die.

QUATRAIN
A quatrain is a four-lined, rhyming poem or stanza. Quatrains have several possible rhyme schemes. The first is designed as two couplets joined together with the a a b b pattern. Other rhyme patterns are a b a b, a b b a, and a b c b.

Example: "Weather"
Evening red and morning gray (a)
Set the traveler on his way (a)
But evening gray and morning red (b)
Bring the rain upon his head (b)

HAIKU
Usually about nature, this style from Japan consists of three unrhymed lines. The first and last line contain five syllables and the middle line has seven syllables. These are easy in theory to fill in the syllables, but it can be hard for the students to actually make them meaningful.

FREE VERSE AND NARRATIVE
There is no fixed pattern, and it can, but does not have to, use rhyming words. Lyric poems focus on feelings and visualizations rather than on a story. Narrative poems tell a story.

"CHILD OF OUR TIME"[121]

I am a child of our time two thousand one
Hearing all my life it's time for action
Don't really care where I spend my last coin
I need followers and transactions

Sea level rising, I show my grief
By posting about the global warming
It was years ago I lost my belief
My generation equals performing

Strangers are now the eyes over a mask
Socially isolated, when's the end?
Watching the capitol under attack
Today inhumanity is a trend

I learned very fast some men can be vile
Like the one time, my friend went on a date
If she knew what he hid behind that smile
The lunch would not have ended with the rape

Child of our time, generation aware
I lived it and I'm now used to despair

---

[121] This gem by Hanna Appelgren was written for NDSCS Creative Writing (Eng211) class in the Spring of 2021. This is licensed CC-BY-NC-SA.

PROFILE

On the cover of most magazines are people posing and photoshopped. Profiles[122] are the textual piece that's written about that person in the magazine. *Rolling Stone* might do a profile piece on the most influential band at the time, *Glamour* might have a profile piece on some actress who has a movie coming out, and even *Hunting* might have a profile piece on the newest species to watch out for.

The best profile pieces typically include interviewee statistics, intriguing quotes from that interview woven in with a summary of the interview, concluding analysis of what the interviewer thought of the whole interview, as well as background information on the interviewee before or during the interviewer's body paragraphs.

PROFILE CREATION

A good profile piece requires a well-rounded person; these are people who are fleshed out in detail, with, for example, a back story that explains their motivations. The following takes you through the steps to create a well-rounded profile piece – it starts on the outside and works its way to the insides of the person.

THE BASICS

Start out with writing down some of the basic facts: Is your character male, female, transgender? Where was your character born? How old are they? What is their current job? What are their interests outside their job? Who do they love? And who did they used to love? Who are their enemies and friends?

PROFILE'S APPEARANCE

The appearance of a person is important but remember as a writer you are describing the appearance, and much will be left to the readers' imagination. You should decide the physical attributes of your profile person. At the least you should consider:

- Height – are they tall, short, average?
- Weight – are they overweight, underweight, average?
- Skin tone, hair and eye color
- Distinguishing features – birthmarks, scars, tattoos
- Hair color – brunette, blonde?
- Hair length – short, long, shoulder length?

Some of these attributes will be worked into the writing early on to allow the reader to form an image of the character in their "mind's eye."

ACCESSORIES & CLOTHING

Think about the things your character wears, carries, and uses and whether any should be distinctive. Think of Mr. T's gold chains, Tupac's bandana, or Carrie's heels

---

[122] "Character Creation." *Wikibooks, The Free Textbook Project*. 17 Aug 2010, 15:00 UTC. 16 May 2016, 15:18 <https://en.wikibooks.org/w/index.php?title=CharacterCreation&oldid=1913045>. Licensed CC-BY-SA.

in *Sex in the City*! These are all iconic accessories. People in real life tend to favor certain items and these items are part of how we recognize them and think of them.

PROFILE BACKGROUND

The background is essential, even if it is not actually detailed. As well as making the profile more interesting and adding depth to the story, the writer can use the background to ensure the profile person's behavior remains consistent. If the writer has written up the background and stated that the character is claustrophobic, then the readers are more likely to understand why the profiled person doesn't like MRIs if the interviewer asks them about medical issues the interviewee has had.

HERITAGE

Your profile person's heritage (and current nationality) could affect other aspects of the profile piece or questions the writer will ask. But equally you should strive to avoid the stereotypes – Germans aren't all mean, Italians aren't all about love and pasta. Sometimes discovering the opposite of the stereotypical view will surprise and interest your reader. How about a German who doesn't drink beer?

PROFILE'S PERSONALITY

Is your profile person mean, nice, funny? That can be determined by their personality... Most people have a mixture of a few personalities. The caring mother mentioned above might be a Type-A scrapbooker and a wine lover. The busy doctor might compete in triathlons and have three pit bulls who she/he puts into beauty competitions. The custodian may be a collector of vintage motorcycles, obsess over a particular hockey team, and spoil his/her granddaughters. It is your job as the profile writer to ask questions that lead to these findings. Here are a few questions to ask:
- What adjectives would your friends use to describe you?
- What hobbies do you have?
- What would your "best day" consist of?
- What is on your Bucket List?
- Describe yourself in one sentence.
- What's something weird in your fridge right now?
- What three items would you want on a deserted island?

WANT.AN.EXAMPLE?
WANT.A.SAMPLE?

"SHE 'WANTS TO BE A ZOMBIE IN A FUTURE LIFE'."[123]

When she was born, I called her "that girl." Apparently, I wasn't too keen on having another kid around. I had the place to myself for three years, so, I guess I had territorial issues.

She was chubby = "Just say I was a fat kid already." She still claims that her baby gut never went away; in college, it was expanded with her addiction to diesel Pepsi. Since then, she's given up that all-out sugar and fills the baby gut with beer. "It's the only right thing to do."

She also felt the oddness, once the other siblings were born, of being the middle child = "It sucks." Alisa was accused of things the rest of us did, which was not cool, but it happened. Of all of us, she was an easy target; she feels guilt quicker ("It's that damn Catholicism at worked!") and had a very secretive rebel side that no one knew of until later. Did she really start smoking at age 14? Yep. And drinking at 15? Yes. But we didn't suspect it.

We lived together when she decided to go to NDSU. At that point, I was a clean freak and she wasn't, but when I ended up on my own later, teaching & exhausted, we would switch spots. Now, she's almost got OCD ("I like things done in 5s; when people touch the volume in my car, I have to ask them to do it in units of 5."). And what adds to it is her English degree. We both get easily irritated with spelling and punctuation errors.

With that English degree came more awkwardness of what to do with it. She's very creative but lacks confidence. And she's not a huge book reader, either, which shocks most. Her most recently read book was *The Zombie Survival Guide*.

While at times I have felt like a mom to her, she is my best friend. We look similar, but her very blue eyes and naturally brown hair make her look wiser and more authentic ("Do people think I'm older than you because I'm angry?" Me: "I think it's your hair color."). She's brutal and fun and knows how to kick ass. Any mention of zombies or pirates or sharks ("Shark Week! Did you know…") or Peyton Manning, and she'll talk your face off. She's almost gotten two nicknames related to her storytelling skills = Sideline and Bulldozer. She tends not to stay on track, and, yes, she'll bulldoze you over with statistics any time.

She's the glue in our family. I wouldn't be as close to my youngest siblings if it weren't for Alisa. We've been through a lot together, but we stick by each other. We've paid each other's way, financially or otherwise ("Red Lobster, courtesy of Ma & Pa!").

At the end of my life, I hope her and I follow-through on our wishes = to have purple hair and wear sweatpants along with t-shirts that say stupid stuff like "Princess" or "Bite Me."

Works Cited

Priebe, Alisa. Personal Interview. 14 Dec 09.

PROPOSAL

Proposals[124] are a technical genre that is found in a few spots of the "real world." For instance, the marriage proposal is one verbal way the genre exists. Otherwise, the paper form exists in companies when, say, a co-worker wants to propose a different way of doing things. If I wanted to teach a different type of course, I might write a proposal to explain what and why I want to teach. Also, this format might be used when you (or any person in the world) want to propose an idea to a bank, or other financial institution, in order to get funding.

Define your audience. You need to make sure that you think about your audience and what they might already know or not know about your topic before you begin writing. This will help you focus your ideas and present them in the most effective way. It's a good idea to assume that your readers will be busy, reading (or even skimming) in a rush, and not predisposed to grant your ideas any special consideration. Efficiency and persuasiveness will be key.

Define your issue. It is clear to you what the issue is, but is that also clear to your reader? Also, does your reader believe you really know what you are talking about? By setting your issue properly, you start convincing the reader that you are the right person to take care of it. Think about the following when you plan this part:
- Has anyone ever tried to deal with this issue before?
- If yes: has it worked? Why?
- If no: why not?

Define your solution. This should be straightforward and easy to understand. Once you set the issue you're addressing, how would you like to solve it? Get it as narrow (and doable) as possible. ASK: Is the solution you're offering logical and feasible? What's the timeline for your implementation?

Include a schedule and budget. Your proposal represents an investment. In order to convince your readers that you're a good investment, provide as much detailed, concrete information about your timeline and budget as possible.
- When do you envision the project starting? At what pace will it progress? How does each step build on the other? Can certain things be done simultaneously?
- Make sure your proposal makes sense financially. If you're proposing an idea to a company or a person, consider their budget. If they can't afford your proposal, it's not an adequate one. If it does fit their budget, be sure to include why it's worth their time and money.

---

[124] "How to Write a Proposal." Co-authored by Megan Morgan, PhD. 11 June 2019. https://www.wikihow.com/Write-a-Proposal.

DORM BUILDING KITCHEN AMENITIES BY REECE[125]

To: North Dakota State College of Science - Residential Life
From: Reece Henri
Date: 04/22/2021
RE: Dorm Building Kitchen Amenities

I am coming to you with this proposal to try and make it easier for students to cook food for themselves without having to leave their dorm building. None of the kitchens on campus - the one on the southside, the one in Robertson, or the one in Nordgaard - have any sort of kitchen necessities such as pots and pans. I have a proposal that will hopefully make it much easier for students to make their own meals if they wish to do so.

Introduction:
My plan is to simply equip each kitchen in every dorm building with the items necessary for students who wish to make food for themselves. Most students don't think about buying pots and pans when they move into college because they figure that they will normally just eat in the Student Center, so they won't need them. Later, some of those students find that they would like to get together with their friends and cook some food, but none of them have the items to do so. For some college students, having bonding time with their friends in the kitchen is very important, but without the means to be in the kitchen due to the lack of equipment, it becomes harder to do.

Audience:
This proposal is directed mostly towards the North Dakota State College of Science Residential Life office, although I do think that if it were to expand to all schools without proper equipment in their kitchens, that would be amazing.

The End Product:
The direct result of having on campus kitchens equipped with necessary kitchen items would be that the students have more fun being in the kitchen and hanging out with friends. Students would spend more time mingling in the kitchen, making friends and creating memories. Instead of students spending money on take-out food or skipping meals because they don't like what Flickertail has to offer for meals, students would be able to make their own food that they know they like and possibly have leftovers from.

Costs and Supplies:
One 17-piece Chef's Classic Stainless Steel Cookware Set costs about $260.00. For the three dorm buildings on campus, that would total to about $780.00. A 23-piece

---

kitchen utensil set costs about $23.00, which would total up to $69.00. These two things together, which is just the basics compared to most at-home kitchens, would be $849.00 total for all three buildings. I would say that at max, it would be no more than $900.00 after getting extra things like sheet pans, cupcake tins, cake pans, etc.

Tentative Schedule of the Proposal:
This is a one step process that will take hardly any time
- Buy the items above before students arrive in the fall, then put those items into the kitchens

REPORT

A report is a very technical document that presents information in an objective way – it's like the polar opposite of an essay or memoir or story. No fluff. Low on creativity. Be precise.

TYPES OF REPORTS

- Progress: explains one's progress with a project or course materials
- Incident: explains what happened during an incident
- Periodic: Reports issued at regular intervals.
- Analytic: shares statistics, predictions, and solutions, so that a person/group can evaluate the action plan
- Proposal:[126] problem-solving reports that include an overview and solution

HOW TO WRITE A REPORT[127]

To have an effective report, try these steps:

1. Choose the main objective – stay focused and engage the readers with clarity
2. Analyze your audience – change the data, vocabulary, and supporting materials depending on the target readers. If you understand your audience, you can add some personal touch and suit the preferences of particular people
3. Work on the report format – learn how to start off a report and how to finalize it effectively
4. Collect the data – add the facts, figures, and data to add credibility
5. Structure the report – they look like an elongated memo
6. Ensure good readability – make navigation easy by adding visuals, graphics, proper formatting with subtitles, and bullet points. Shorter paragraphs are better than long bulks of text
7. Do the editing.

Scan the report to make sure everything is included and makes sense. Read the report from beginning to end, trying to imagine that you're a reader that has never heard this information before.

A good question to ask yourself is, "If I were someone reading this report for the first time, would I feel like I understood the topic after I finished reading?

---

[126] Oooh, look at the overlap between genres here!

[127] Listmann, Emily (co-authored). "How to Write a Report." *Wikihow.* http://www.wikihow.com/Write-A-Report 12 Sept 09. Licensed CC-BY-NC-SA.

FAKE PROGRESS REPORT ON A FAKE COMPANY

To: John Booger, Bell State Flank
From: Sybil Priebe,[128] Owner of T&P
Date: July 29, 2015
Subject: Progress Report regarding Clothing Line Expansion & Creation

The following is the second progress report concerning the expansion and creation of our clothing line. Work has proceeded satisfactorily in July according to the plans we laid out and had approved in May.

REVIEW OF WORK COMPLETED
In my last report (June 1) we reported that we had successfully got bids with a fashion company in Minneapolis (JuneBug Inc.) to start designing a new line of jeans. The expansion part of the project was also taken care of by JuneBug Inc. as they have opened up their warehouse of designer t-shirts to our company. The bid we received from them for the new line of jeans included the expansion into designer t-shirts.

To break it down, work completed from May 1 –July 1 included:
- Sending out bids to various venders of t-shirts and jeans' clothing lines
- Preparing the current store merchandise by having a tremendously successful clearance sale
- Conducting two employee meetings to make them aware of the creation and expansion
- Received feedback from employees on how to sell new merchandise effectively
- By June 25, we had received various shipments of the designer t-shirts from JuneBug. In total, we received 50 t-shirts in that shipment alone. We had underestimated their quick delivery of those items, so we had some employees spend overtime hours that weekend moving around our floor plan to make room for the new merchandise.
- Tagging and steam-cleaning of designer t-shirts
- Creation of posters in order to promote the new expansion of t-shirts
- Hiring a temporary person for the moving of the floor plan in the coming months

PROBLEMS WITH THE EXPANSION
As mentioned above, we still have little space for the new merchandise, and the new jeans line has not even gotten here yet. We have already attempted to solve this glitch by contacting our floor planner rep, and she has ordered new organizers for our t-shirts and jeans that will most likely fit in the store without causing major readjusting to the floor plan. If the organizers she is sending do not work out with the store's floor plan, I

---

may have to contact you regarding an additional loan for expansion of the store to the attic. The attic itself is empty; the walls would simply need to be finished and painted.

OTHER POSSIBLE PROBLEMS:
As I mentioned in the June 1 report, we hope to have a huge sell out of the new jeans line, but if the merchandise is not as popular as we hope it to be, we may need to reconsider expansion of the store as well as using JuneBug Inc. as our distributor.

WORK REMAINING
Not only do we need to check on the idea of renovating the attic for space (as a backup for the space issue on the main floor), but we also need to receive the jeans order from JuneBug Inc. At the last conference call with them, they stated that once they received our exact number of each size and style they would process our designs. We've also ordered their own designs (JuneBug Bottoms), and that order is due within the next two months which is why the space issue is something we should address now.

OTHER WORK REMAINING:
- Advertise JuneBug Bottoms
- Conduct employee meetings and fittings of both JuneBug Bottoms' styles and our own designs
- Paint the east wall of the store with sizes and their corresponding names of styles: Annie (0-2), Lela (4-6), Mandy (8-10), Carrie (12-14), Betty (16-18), Tori (20)

CONCLUSION
By September 15, I hope to be able to send you another progress report. By that time, we should have received the organizers from our floor plan designer, and we'll be able to inform you as to whether those organizers will work or whether we need to look into using the attic, etc. as mentioned previously. By September 15, we will have also had more contact with JuneBug Inc. and know exact dates for the shipment and delivery of both their jean designs and our jean designs. And, lastly, the store will have been painted then to make way for the store's new expansion of a jeans line.

Thank you again for your confidence in our company. Please contact me with any questions.

RESUME

A résumé[129] is a summary of your educational background, employment experience, and skills. It is a way to communicate your qualifications for a desired position to an employer. Your résumé is your tool to market yourself and the key to getting an interview. Essentially, you are creating your résumé as a pitching, selling, and branding tool of yourself to potential employers.

There is no "best way" to write a résumé. However, there are some general guidelines, such as clarity, accuracy and neatness, that should be followed. It is important to choose a résumé style and format that will work best for you and the job you are applying for. How do you decide what approach will be the best? Here are some questions you can ask yourself to help with the decision:

- What are the employer's needs and interests for the position for which I am applying?
- What are my strengths for the job and how can I emphasize them?
- How can I format and organize the content and graphics of my résumé to show what I have to offer?

TYPES OF RÉSUMÉS

There are three main types of résumés: Experiential/chronological, skills/functional, and a combination of the two. What format to use is up to you and your situation. Each type emphasizes a different component of the résumé. Experiential résumés emphasize work experience, skills résumés emphasize skills and abilities, and combination résumés seek to find a balance between the two. When deciding what type of résumés to create, choose one that is common to your industry. Every industry uses different types of résumés according to what the industry standard is.

EXPERIENTIAL RÉSUMÉS

Experiential résumés list information in reverse chronological order. Most college students will choose to list education first, because students have limited work experience. The most recent degrees are listed first followed by previous degrees. The same format is followed under each heading. Skills gained from each job are listed under each job title, along with accomplishments and responsibilities. Experiential résumés are useful for establishing a work history and for showcasing accomplishments made at each career position. Experiential résumés are the most common type of résumé and are a simple way to detail responsibilities held at different jobs.

---

[129] "Professional and Technical Writing/Career/Resumes." *Wikibooks, The Free Textbook Project.* 16 Aug 2019, 12:37 UTC. 10 Oct 2019, 17:09 <https://en.wikibooks.org/w/index.php?title=Professional_and_Technical_Writing/Career/Resumes&oldid=35634 57>. Licensed CC-BY-SA.

Ethel Aardvark   **701-555-5555**

900 Perfection Road
Bingo, MN 58075
Phone: (o) 701-671-5555, (h/c) 701-555-5555
Email: ethel.aardvark@gmail.com

EDUCATION

Some Midwest State University: Boonies, ND.
B.A. in Cool Education, May, 1999.

EXPERIENCE

Crazy Scholars Program – Online: Some Texas University, Spring 1999.
+Duties: Preparing activities, tutoring students via email (revising and assessing stuff), and keeping office chat room hours.

Research Palace: Mini-Apple, MN, 1990-1999.
+Duties: Assisted a regional independent student newspaper with general customer service and photography, as well as assisted in editing/proofreading.

PROFESSIONAL GROUPS

-ISP (Independent Student Paper) Coalition.

INTERESTS

-Anything Blasphemous and/or Cool
-Hypertext & Web Site building
-Technical and Professional Document/ Design

REFERENCES

Mr. Stevie Nicks, Manager
(Retired) Research Palace, stevie_nicks@aol.com

Professor Reed Books
Cool Research Department, Some Midwest State University.

SKILLS RÉSUMÉS

A skills (or functional) résumé organizes information around types of skills and abilities. Headings may include "Computer Skills," "Foreign Languages," and "Leadership Experience." A skills résumé will list the skill and then explain when and how that particular skill was used. Skills résumés are useful for several reasons: they avoid repeating the same information under each job title; they emphasize skills and abilities (a college graduate's work history may be from only part-time work, and a skills résumé will merely mention these positions); lastly, they hide gaps in an applicant's work history

Anytime attention should be focused away from work experience – due to a gap in experience, etc. – a skills résumé is recommended.

Rodger Bern

6767 Juniper Drive – Apt. 4
Lovely Lane, FL 50005
Phone: (h/c) 218-555-5555
Email: RB1999@gmail.com

EDUCATION

Florida State University.
B.A. in Construction; May 2010.

PROFESSIONAL GROUPS

- National Honor Society
- National Construction Alliance
- Students of Latino Pride

SKILLS

Computer Skills:
- PlanGrid - Project Designware, Bid Management , Field service management, and Safety Reporting
- Microsoft Office
- Construction Takeoff Software
- Estimation of Materials Costware
- PMS: Project Management and Scheduling

Foreign Language Skills:
- Fluent Spanish in speaking and writing
- Fluent Italian in speaking
- Fluent English in speaking and writing

Leadership Skills: Conflict Resolution, Group Work Delegation

REFERENCES

Professor Tresha Bloom

Images of both "Ethel" and "Rodger" were found via Unsplash/Pixlr.com.

COMBINATION RÉSUMÉS

A combination résumé lists skills and abilities first, but also lists accomplishments and responsibilities under specific job titles and experiences. A combination résumé allows an applicant to highlight specific skills that may be desired by the employer while also emphasizing job experience. Combination résumés are useful for applicants with an extensive job history in a highly specialized field. For example, applicants in computer programming may want to highlight their computer language skills before detailing their computer programming experience.

CREATIVE / VISUAL RESUME

Ultra-creative resumes are rare; however, they will definitely set you apart from other applicants. The following example took Ethel's information from the chronological resume first showcased in this chapter and made it much more VISUALLY pleasing.

Ethel Aardvark
DIGITAL EDUCATOR

Skills

- Tutoring Optimization
- Education Research
- Grant Writer
- Customer Service
- Photography / Newspaper Experience

Experience

ISP (Independent Student Paper) Coalition, part-time; 2005-current.

Crazy Scholars Program – Online: Some Texas University, Spring 1999.

Research Palace: Mini-Apple, MN, 1990-1999.

Education

Some Midwest State University: Boonies, ND. B.A. in Cool Education, May, 1999.

About Me

I am a digital education expert with an emphasis in tutoring optimization, educational research/grants, and other customer service geared at student learning.

Contact

Phone: (h/c) 701-555-5555
Email:
ethel.aardvark@gmail.com

This creative resume was put together using the web site Canva.

THE PIECES OF A RÉSUMÉ

When writing your résumé, you must make decisions about such things as what to say, how to organize etc. Think about your readers. What will they be looking for? The following sections provide your general style when writing your résumé:

- **Personal Information**: Include your name, address, and professional email address. Many employers like to see a home or cell phone number on the résumé as well.
- **Career Objective** - *Optional*: Many people believe that they need to have an objective listed underneath their contact information; however, the truth is that maybe objectives should not part of your résumé because they are limiting.

- **Education**: Education should be included immediately after your identifying information unless you have had significant work experiences in the field for which you are applying. In that case, education should be placed at the end of the résumé.
- **Work Experience**: Include information about your employment history within your résumé. For each job, include the company name, location, and specific dates employed. In addition, employment should be listed in reverse chronological order. You should also list some of the knowledge you gained from your work experience and some of the responsibilities you were given.
  - When speaking of past tasks, you held at a previous job, verbs should be in the past tense form. If you are speaking of job tasks you currently preform, use the present tense. Use action verbs! Use a thesaurus as a resource in order to not repeat verbs.
    - Use Accomplishment Statements
      - Increase productivity and quality... Increased sales...
      - Improve communications and information flow...
      - Streamlined operations...
      - Developed new administrative procedure that...
      - Implemented a new program in...
      - Reduced cost of...
- **Achievements**: Awards, recognitions, or other special circumstances should be included if they are outstanding and directly related to the job for which you are applying.
- **Volunteer Experience**.
- **Skills**: Be sure to include any special skills that you have, such as being fluent in another language or being an expert in Microsoft applications.
- **References**: When choosing a reference or references, make sure that you can trust them to answer honestly. Be sure to ask them if they are willing to be a reference before giving their information to a potential employer. Shy away from putting "references upon request" because that's one extra step an employer has to take; make it easy for them to hire you.

RÉSUMÉ DESIGN TIPS

- **Simplicity:** Do not clutter the page with unnecessary information. Use bulleted statements to make achievements quick and easy to read.
- **Eye Catching:** See creative resume in this chapter.
- **Format:** Typically, résumés should not be no longer than one page, unless stated otherwise. However, there are many different opinions on this, however.
- **Consistency:** Use the same formatting for similar sections on your résumé. Use line breaks, indents, and font variations to organize relevant information into sections.
- **Font:** Be sure to use fonts that are easy to read.

Whether a book or movie[130] is a rotten tomato or a brilliant work of art, if people are reading or watching it, it's worth critiquing. A decent book/movie/TV show review should entertain, persuade, and inform, providing an original opinion without giving away too much of the plot.

A *great* review can be a work of art in its own right. Read on to learn how to analyze a book/movie, come up with an interesting thesis and write a review as entertaining as your source material.

Gather basic facts about the book/movie/TV show and Take Notes. You can do this before or after you watch/read the movie/book, but you should definitely do it before you write the review, because you'll need to weave the facts into your review as you write. Here's what you need to know: The title and year; the director's or author's name; the names of the lead actors/characters; the genre.

Start with a compelling fact or opinion on the book/movie. You want to get the reader hooked immediately. This sentence needs to give them a feel for your review and the work – is it good, great, terrible, or just okay? – and keep them reading.

Give a clear, well-established opinion early on. Don't leave the reader guessing whether you like the book/movie or not. Let them know early on, so that you can spend the rest of the time "proving" your rating.
- Using stars, a score out of 10 or 100, or the simple thumbs-up and thumbs-down is a quick way to give your thoughts. You then write about why you chose that rating.
- **Great Movie:** "It is the rare movie that succeeds on almost every level, where each character, scene, costume, and joke firing on all cylinders to make a film worth repeated viewings."
- **Bad Movie:** "It doesn't matter how much you enjoy kung-fu and karate films: with *47 Ronin,* you're better off saving your money, your popcorn, and time."
- **Okay Movie:** "I loved the wildly uneven *Interstellar* far more than I should have, but that doesn't mean it is perfect. Ultimately, the utter awe and spectacle of space swept me through the admittedly heavy-handed plotting and dialogue."

Write your review. This is where taking notes during the movie really pays off. No one cares about your opinion if you can't give facts that support your argument.

Move beyond the obvious plot analysis. Plot is just one piece of a movie and shouldn't dictate your entire review. Some movies don't have great or compelling plots, but that doesn't mean the movie itself is bad. Other things to focus on include:
- **Cinematography:** "*Her* is a world drenched in color, using bright, soft reds and oranges alongside calming whites and grays that both builds, and slowly strip

---

[130] "How to Write a Movie Review." Co-authored by wikiHow Staff | Updated: September 17, 2019. https://www.wikihow.com/Write-a-Movie-Review Under an CC-BY-NC-SA License, wikiHow's text content is free to modify, republish and share.

away, the feelings of love between the protagonists. Every frame feels like a painting worth sitting in."

- **Tone:** "Despite discussing mental health, Jenny Lawson's witty script keeps humor alive in her books.
- **Music and Sound:** "*No Country for Old Men*'s bold decision to skip music entirely pays off in spades. The eerie silence of the desert, punctuated by the brief spells of violent, up-close-and-personal sound effects of hunter and hunted, keeps you constantly on the edge of your seat."
- **Acting:** "Gaga tears into the role with all the power and emotional intuition she brings to her music."[131]

Bring your review full circle in the ending. Give the review some closure, usually by trying back to your opening fact. Remember, people read reviews to decide whether or not they should watch a movie/book/TV show. End on a sentence that tells them.

QUESTIONS:

○ Have you used certain web sites – Yelp, Amazon, LinkedIn, Angie's List – for reviewing work or an item? What makes a good review?

WANT.AN.EXAMPLE?
WANT.A.SAMPLE?

EXAMPLE: REMEMBER THE TITANS REVIEW[132]

The movie "Remember the Titans," is about the segregation and football. It starts when two different schools, black and white students, combine their football team. The season before their senior year they all must go to a summer football camp together and join as one strong team to win the state champion. However, during this time they are not fond of each other and fight all the time. The coaches bring them together as one and each game is an adventure especially playing all white teams. In the end of the movie one of the captains gets severely hurt and cannot finish the game, but at the end the team finishes the job and takes home the champion.

In my opinion, I think that this movie is very good. It teaches about segregation. It's about leadership, sports, and commitment. I think a huge factor that plays in it is race and no matter what color you are everybody is the same. It is very inspirational, and it is based on a true story. In the movie there was a lot of injustice about race and it's a great story. I think it brings faith back in humanity.

My opinion early in the movie was that there was a lot of judgement between the whites and black and it made me very emotional to see how it was back them for an example how the blacks were treated and I thought that it was going to stay like that for the whole movie. However, in the end it came out to have a great outcome.

---

[131] Travers, Peter. "'House of Gucci' review: Lady Gaga puts real sizzle in the Oscar race." *GMA*. https://abcnews.go.com/GMA/Culture/house-gucci-review-lady-gaga-puts-real-sizzle/story?id=81327732

[132] This example by Shaylynn N. was created in the Spring of 2020; its licensed CC-BY-NC-SA.

Finally, my review of the movie would be a 10/10 just because it teaches so much about history and I love how it is based on a true story. I would definitely recommend this movie to someone who likes sports because it teaches a lot of leadership and respect to others.

+

 **Adam Cook**
@adam_cook2014

 Follow

My professor handed back our 3 page film essays to my surprise I got a C after class I asked her why "you were supposed to write it about the movie The Emperor of Time.. you wrote it on The Emperor's new Groove but it was kinda good so I didn't fail you" so thats how im doing

10:51 AM - 12 Dec 2017

92,199 Retweets **507,007** Likes

TEXT MESSAGE

Text messaging,[133] or texting, is a method of communication in which short text messages are exchanged using mobile phones.

TEXTESE

The abbreviations and slang associated with text messaging is referred to as textese. The development of textese is often discussed with respect to its history and its parallel development with internet slang as part of internet linguistics. There have been several cases where textese has been used outside of text messages.

In 2003, a 13-year-old student in Scotland handed in an essay written entirely in textese. In 2006, New Zealand's Qualification Authority announced the use of textese would be permitted on national exams. A study by the Pew Research center shows that teens who own cell phones are significantly more likely to incorporate textese into their school writing than teens who do not own cell phones. Furthermore, authoritative reference guides, such as the AP Stylebook and the Merriam Webster Dictionary, also include textese.

IMPACT OF TEXTESE

The impact of textese has also been described as a natural phenomenon. For centuries, people have been innovating language.

"But it is merely the latest manifestation of the human ability to be linguistically creative and to adapt language to suit the demands of diverse settings. There is no disaster pending... In texting what we are seeing, in a small way, is language in evolution." – David Crystal, 2b or Not 2b

One study of children ages 10 to 12 found positive correlation between the use of textese and literacy. Other studies have simply shown that there is no negative correlation.

Even with these studies, some sources, such as the Former National Writing Project Executive Director Richard Sterling, feel that students are simply not given enough credit. Students themselves agree that they know when it is appropriate to use textese in their communications.

QUESTIONS:

- o What have you learned about texting from your friends'/family's text messages? Which ones are the most effective?
- o Do we have to "read" text message differently than other genres? What do we have to analyze that's different?

---

[133] "Lentis/Sociology of Texting." Wikibooks, The Free Textbook Project. 23 Aug 2014, 15:09 UTC. 31 Oct 2021, 14:09 <https://en.wikibooks.org/w/index.php?title=Lentis/Sociology_of_Texting&oldid=2694127>.

Tweets might be the teeniest, tinest genre of all.[134] So, maybe this chapter should be teeny, tiny, too?

MICROBLOGS = TWEETS[135]

Microblogs are a relatively new phenomenon and are a special form of blogging. The most famous microblog is Twitter, but also alternatives like Tumblr or Google Buzz exist. The main idea behind a microblog is to restrict the size of a message to 140[136] characters. This comes from its original connection to texting (SMS). In today's society with its general tendency toward information overflow this is a welcome trend. This is also why it is very popular with mobile devices.

Microblogging is essentially a broadcast medium, meaning you write a message, which then will be broadcast to all your followers. It is not unusual that you also follow your followers. It can not only be used to exchange textual messages, but also links, images, and videos.

THE GOAL OF A TWEET:

The goal is brevity with hefty content. How can you say what you want to say in the smallest space possible? And[137], in order to find other thoughts like yours, use a hashtag.

WANT.AN.EXAMPLE?
WANT.A.SAMPLE?

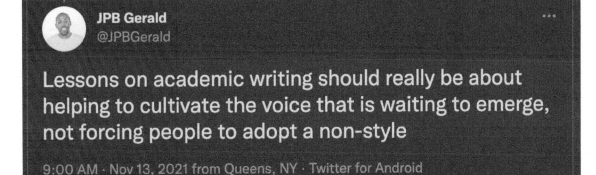

JPB Gerald
@JPBGerald

Lessons on academic writing should really be about helping to cultivate the voice that is waiting to emerge, not forcing people to adopt a non-style

9:00 AM · Nov 13, 2021 from Queens, NY · Twitter for Android

---

[134] Okay, text messages give tweets a run for their money.
[135] "Social Web/Blogs." *Wikibooks, The Free Textbook Project*. 17 Dec 2014, 14:26 UTC. 8 May 2019, 19:17
<https://en.wikibooks.org/w/index.php?title=Social_Web/Blogs&oldid=2748518>. Licensed CC-BY-SA.
[136] Since this nugget was written, Twitter has doubled the character count to 280.
[137] A lot of rules fly right out the window with tweets due to the space allowed.

KILLA KUSH
@killakushla

My prof said "You are not entitled to your opinion. You are only entitled to what you can argue for."

This hit me especially w/ all the fake woke ppl online. It's important to know what you truly stand for, the facts and rational behind it. Otherwise, it's meaningless.

1/21/18, 10:30 AM

CHAPTER 5: STRATEGIES

To be completely honest with y'all, this chapter might not be focused on since the book is primarily focused on GENRES. So, most of this chapter might only be in the EXPANDED version? Or it might only include the strategy of argument?

You're ready to write. You've fired up your laptop, created a new page, and are ready to roll. But, after staring at the blinking cursor for a few minutes, you have no idea where to begin. No need to panic. Now is the time to consider the rhetorical situation – the purpose, audience, author, context, and text – and select a writing strategy to help develop and organize your work. Maybe you want to use narration to tell a story or description to use details in explaining how something works. This next set of chapters will explore how these strategies and others can help make your writing clear and effective.

As you read, ask yourself what sort of **structure** you've seen these strategies (or modes) used in. What kinds of **content** have you see when it comes to these strategies (or modes)? Do you see a strict or flexible structure used? Do you see creative content or technical content used?

Note: Strategies are fluid guidelines that can change or combine according to the goals of your writing.

WANT.AN.EXAMPLE?
WANT.A.SAMPLE?

"THE FIVE MODES/STRATEGIES IN FIVE PARAGRAPHS... WITH THE THEME OF SHOPPING."

NARRATION:
My love for shopping started when I was very young and has followed me throughout my teen and college years. Back when I was younger, and didn't have a credit card, I had to rely on my mom to take me shopping. I remember getting very excited when she and my dad would announce a trip to Fargo because that meant we'd go to the mall. Although I wasn't' a shop-a-holic back then, I did love the simple act of wandering through racks of clothes as well as trying on a pile of them even if they didn't fit. When I was in high school, I started shopping on my own at places that suited my budget. The local thrift stores became my favorite places even thought my mom disapproved of us buying secondhand items. Once I came to Fargo to go to college, I still shopped at thrift stores (there were so many more up here!), and slowly, as my income increased as well as my amount of credit, I made my way to the mall more often and started online shopping too. Although I have expanded the variety of stores I shop at, my sister and I still to this day love going to thrift stores to find cheap tees, funky bags, and weird furniture.

ILLUSTRATION OR EXAMPLE:
There are many different places a person can shop for clothing at, but it depends on what you are looking for. If you want vintage, I suggest these stores in Fargo: Savers, Dakota Boys Ranch, and the Salvation Army. If you aren't intimidated by online shopping, try eBay.

For basics, I go to Target first, then Old Navy, and then the Gap. This list goes from cheapest to most expensive, in my opinion.

COMPARISON/CONTRAST:
While the outcome is the same, online shopping is quite different from physically shopping in a mall.
[Online Shopping- Weather doesn't matter; don't have to walk around and get crabby, more stores to look at that aren't in your area.
Physically Shopping- exercise, alone time away from home, get to try on things.]

CAUSE AND EFFECT:
The effect of a good shopping trip is both beneficial and detrimental to a shop-a-holic.
[Good: exercise, new clothes, good attitude, research for future purchase. Bad: costs money, wastes time that could be used doing something else, and could make you stressed out from spending money or trying on clothes that don't fit well.]

DEFINITION (SOMEWHAT ARGUMENTATIVE):
The definition of "window shopping" is not necessarily walking by a window, peering in to see what's for sale. Oh, no. Window shopping can be expanded to simply mean "shopping by looking and not necessarily buying." One can window shop and purchase items or one can window shop for days without buying a dang thing. Window shopping can be done at yard sales, thrift stores, malls, department stores, and, yes, while walking down Broadway peaking at window displays. [etc.]

ARGUMENT

We don't always argue to win. Yes, you read that correctly. Argumentation isn't always about being "right." We argue to express opinions and explore new ideas. When writing an argument, your goal is to convince an audience that your opinions and ideas are worth consideration and discussion.

What distinguishes an argument from a descriptive essay or "report" is that the argument must take a stance; if you're merely summarizing "both sides" of an issue or pointing out the "pros and cons," you're not really writing an argument.

Academic arguments usually "articulate an opinion." This opinion is always carefully defended with good reasoning and supported by plenty of research. Research? Yes, research! Indeed, part of learning to write effective arguments is finding reliable sources (or other documents) that lend credibility to your position. It's not enough to say, "capital punishment is wrong because that's the way I feel."

Instead, you need to adequately support your claim by finding:
- facts
- statistics
- quotations from recognized authorities, and
- other types of evidence

You won't always win, and that's fine. The goal of an argument is simply to:
- make a claim
- support your claim with the most credible reasoning and evidence you can muster
- hope that the reader will at least understand your position
- hope that your claim is taken seriously

WHAT IS AN ARGUMENT?

Billboards, television advertisements, documentaries, political campaign messages, and even bumper stickers are often arguments – these are messages trying to convince an audience to do something. But be aware that an academic argument is different. An academic argument requires a clear structure and use of outside evidence.

KEY FEATURES OF AN ARGUMENT

- **Clear Structure:** Includes a claim, reasons/evidence, counterargument, and conclusion.

---

[138] This chapter's contents come from the original chapter on Argument in the first edition of *Writing Unleashed.*
[139] "What is an Argument?" *Wikibooks, The Free Textbook Project.* Last edited 27 Nov 14. Accessed 10 May 17. https://en.m.wikibooks.org/wiki/Rhetoric_and_Composition/Argument Text is available under the Creative Commons Attribution-ShareAlike License.

- **Claim:** Your arguable point (most often presented as your thesis statement).
- **Reasons & Evidence:** Strong reasons and materials that support your claim.
- **Consideration of other Positions:** Acknowledge and refute possible counterarguments.
- **Persuasive Appeals:** Use of appeals to emotion, character, and logic.
- Organizing an Argument

The great thing about the argument structure is its amazingly versatility. Once you become familiar with this basic structure of the argumentative essay, you will be able to clearly argue about almost anything! Next up is information all about the basic structure...

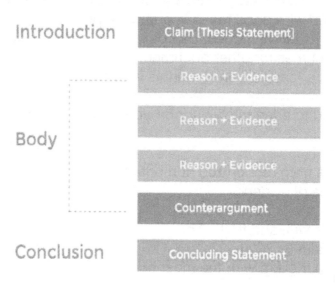

140

A NOTE ABOUT OBJECTIVE LANGUAGE

Some instructors tell you to avoid using "I" and "My" (subjective) statements in your argument, but it's not so black and white. Perhaps consider only using "I" or "My" if you are an expert in your field (on a given topic). If you are not an expert, choose more objective language to get your point across.

Consider the following:

I believe that the United States Government is failing to meet the needs of today's average college student through the under-funding of need-based grants, increasingly restrictive financial aid eligibility requirements, and a lack of flexible student loan options.

---

140 Image used in previous OER textbook, *Writing Unleashed*, the non-argumentative one. It was created by Dana Anderson on Piktochart.

"Great," your reader thinks, "Everyone's entitled to their opinion."

Now let's look at this sentence again, but without the "I" at the beginning. Does the same
sentence become a strong statement of fact without your "I" tacked to the front?

The United States Government is failing to meet the needs of today's average college student through the underfunding of need-based grants, increasingly restrictive financial aid eligibility requirements, and a lack of flexible student loan options.

"Wow," your reader thinks, "that really sounds like a problem."

A small change like the removal of your "I"s and "my"s can make all the difference in how a reader perceives your argument – as such, it's always good to proofread your rough draft and look for places where you could use objective rather than subjective language.

A NOTE ABOUT AUDIENCE WHEN ARGUING

Many topics that are written about in college are very controversial. When approaching a topic, it is critical that you think about all of the implications that your argument makes.

QUESTIONS TO CONSIDER WHEN ARGUING[141]

- How would your relatives/friends/classmates react to the argument? Would they understand the terminology you are using? Does that matter?
- How would you explain your argument or research to a teenager vs someone who is in their 70s? Is there a difference?
- If you are aware that your classmates are more liberal or more conservative in their political standing, does that determine how you will argue your topic? Or does that even matter? If you are aware that your instructor is more liberal or conservative than you are, does that determine how you will argue your topic? Or does that even matter?
- If you were to people-watch at a mall or other space where many people gather, who in the crowd would be your ideal audience and why? Who is not your ideal audience member? Why?

[141] Questions taken from a longer piece by: Jory, Justin. "A Word About Audience." *Open English at Salt Lake Community College*. 01 Aug 2016. https://openenglishatslcc.pressbooks.com/chapter/audience/ Open English @ SLCC by SLCC English Department is licensed under a Creative Commons Attribution-Noncommercial 4.0 International License, except where otherwise noted.

EXAMPLE: "CAN GRAFFITI EVER BE CONSIDERED ART?"[142]

Graffiti is not simply acts of vandalism, but a true artistic form because of personal expression, aesthetic qualities, and movements of style.

Graffiti, like traditional artistic forms such as sculpture, is art because it allows artists to express ideas through an outside medium.

Graffiti must be considered an art form based on judgement of aesthetic qualities. Art professor George C. Stowers argues that "larger pieces require planning and imagination and contain artistic elements like color and composition" ("Graffiti").

Like all artistic forms, Graffiti has evolved, experiencing significant movements or periods.

Often, graffiti is seen as only criminal vandalism, but this is not always the case. The artistic merits of graffiti–expression, aesthetics, and movements–cannot be denied; Graffiti is art.

Works Cited
"Graffiti: Art through Vandalism." Graffiti: Art through Vandalism. N.p., n.d. Web. 29 Sept. 2015.

+

Ashley C. Ford ✔
@iSmashFizzle

A teacher friend went over safety procedures with her class & asked, "If I'm shot, what do you do?" One of her students said, "Avenge you."

9/14/16, 9:22 PM

---

[142] Example used in previous OER textbook, *Writing Unleashed.*

MORE STRATEGIES AND MODES

Here are other strategies and modes you may come across: Informative/Expository, Imaginative/Creative, Technical, Definition, Cause and Effect, Process Analysis, Exemplification, Compare and Contrast, and… Classification and Division. Yes, as the Venn diagram shows below, there are intersections between strategies, modes, and genres.

BLACK: STRATEGIES/MODES   GREY: GENRES

PLEASE NOTE: THESE STRATEGIES, MODES, AND GENRES ARE FLUID AND FLEXIBLE. THEY ARE NOT SET IN STONE.

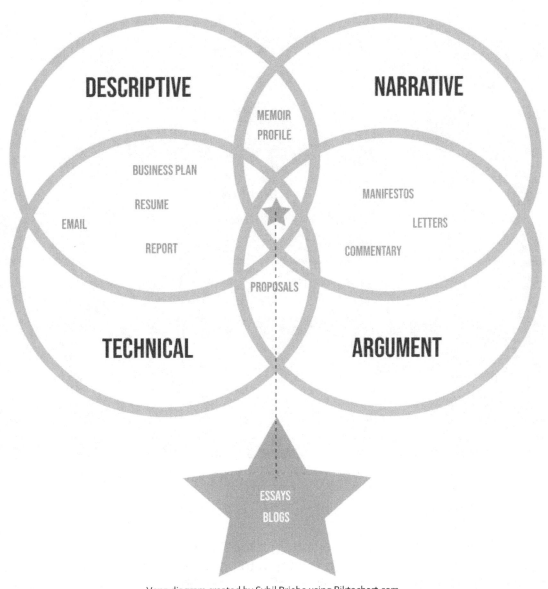

Venn diagram created by Sybil Priebe using Piktochart.com.

qunaributts Seguir

I had a professor in college who used to start solving every problem with the same dialogue.

Proff: What's the first step to solving any problem?
Class: Don't panic.
Proff: And why is that?
Class: Because we know more than we think we do.

I think about that a lot tbh. It didn't occur to me until much later that he meant for us to apply that dialogue outside of the classroom to any problem. Because we always know more than we think we do. We are all an amalgam of random information that ends up being relevant with surprising frequency.

CHAPTER 6: RESEARCH

At some point in your college career, a teacher may throw a research project in your face. The teacher might assign the topic to be researched – "Your question is: Where did the electoral college come from?" – or it might be open-ended, and in that case, you almost have free reign as to what you dive into.

THE STEPS

STEP 0: BACKGROUND

So, what does it really mean to do research?[143] Research is a three-stage process: (1) seeking information that is new to the researcher, (2) interpreting, evaluating, and organizing that information, and (3) reporting that information to others to affect some action.

A more useful approach to teaching students about research, and how to do research, begins with re-thinking how we define research and research skills. If research is the process by which a researcher seeks new information, makes sense of that information, and then reports that information to someone else, then research ought to begin with a question, not an answer. Students need to be taught not to look for answers, but to look for problems that need solving and for questions that need to be answered.

Rather than limiting the conception of research to a search for certain facts or pieces of evidence or to a trip to the library, it needs to include the processes of primary research[144]—research collected directly by the researcher using tools he or she has designed to find the information needed to answer a particular question. I am not suggesting that secondary research[145]—the locating of previously published materials—be eliminated, but that it not be presented as the paramount form of research, as is often done in the research paper. Secondary research is a key part of the research process and usually precedes any primary research. Once a researcher has a question, it's logical to see if and how others might have answered the same question. To be successful, students, and any researchers, must have a working knowledge of the question they are investigating. However, that information serves as a starting point for researchers, who then ask further questions to spur and design their own primary research.

STEP 1: WHY DOES THIS MATTER?

The focus of college composition[146] is the types of writing students will encounter in college and their careers. Most of the majors students choose require them to conduct extensive research all the way through college. So, the students' job is to learn how to do it so as to demonstrate their researching skills and increasing knowledge.

An introduction to college writing is based on understanding that the primary underlying skill of academic writing at the college level lies within analysis and the ability to synthesize information into one's own words, citing sources as needed, with the confidence of one who feels part of a given community. The skills needed for good research-based writing involve reading the work of experts, assimilating that information with one's own brilliant (and evolving) ideas, possibly mirroring some of the

---

[143] Snippet from = Witte, Alison C. "Research Starts with Answers." *Bad Ideas About Writing*. Edited by Cheryl E. Ball and Drew M. Loewe. Morgantown, WV: West Virginia University Libraries, Digital Publishing Institute, 2017. CC-BY.

[144] Primary research is research conducted by the researcher like first-hand interviews and surveys.

[145] Secondary research is sites like Wikipedia that have the primary sources linked or listed, but they provide an overview of the primary research that has already been conducted.

[146] Contributed by Ann Inoshita, Karyl Garland, Kate Sims, Jeanne K. Tsutsui Keuma, and Tasha Williams: Professors at University of Hawaii. Sourced from *University of Hawaii OER*. This story has been licensed under CC-BY 2.0. Updated Sept 9, 2019.

writing that suits each individual student, and becoming a clear, creative, and confident writer in his or her own right.

STEP 2: WHAT IS YOUR TOPIC?

If the research project is open-ended, brainstorm with classmates, friends, tutors, or your teacher to figure out what your topic will be. Will you try to answer what vegans eat and why? Will you look up all the reasons behind teen suicides? Or will you research ways to start your own business?

STEP 3: WHO IS YOUR AUDIENCE?[147]

Are you writing for the classroom and your teacher OR are you writing for the public? If you are writing for a general audience, what is the best way to capture a wide range of readers' interests? Should you provide background information that general readers would not necessarily know?

STEP 4: WHAT TYPES/KINDS OF RESEARCH ARE REQUIRED?

After nailing down a research topic, decide whether to use primary or secondary sources. When it comes to secondary, instructors may want a combination of popular and scholarly. And, lastly, sometimes, your instructor will push you to consider both primary and secondary that come from both popular and scholarly areas.

TYPES OF RESEARCH

- PRIMARY RESEARCH
  - This is conducted first-hand and includes interviews, blogs and forums, surveys and question groups, etc. The key to conducting primary research is accuracy and privacy.
- SECONDARY RESEARCH
  - This is the gathering of information that has previously been analyzed, assessed, or otherwise documented or compiled including: sources (print or electronic) such as books, magazine articles, Wikipedia, reports, video recordings, correspondence, etc.

STEP 5: FINDING QUALITY SECONDARY RESEARCH.

If the research project calls for secondary research, then you'll need to seek out some quality pieces to use. If the research project calls for only primary research, then you'll seek out experts to interview, create surveys for people to take, etc.

KEYWORD SEARCHING:[148] DO IT BETTER![149]

If you start by searching on good old regular Google (seeking out some popular sources), accurate terms or punctuation changes should be used to signal a more specific search or topic and lead to better results. Here are a few helpful tips:

---

[147] Contributed by Ann Inoshita, Karyl Garland, Kate Sims, Jeanne K. Tsutsui Keuma, and Tasha Williams: Professors at University of Hawaii. Sourced from *University of Hawaii OER*. This information has been licensed under CC-BY 2.0. Updated Sept 9, 2019.

[148] These Search Tricks (also called Boolean and/or Proximity Searching) allow you to specify how close a search term appears in relation to another term contained in the resources you find.

[149] Jeffrey, Robin. *About Writing: A Guide. Revised Edition.* OpenOregon. CC-BY.

- Searching a phrase? Put it in quotation marks: "textbook affordability" will get you results for that exact phrase.
- Searching for two terms that you think are related? Use AND (or +) to connect them: education AND racism, or: education + racism, will only bring up results that include both terms
- Using "OR" retrieves articles with an of the terms and broadens the search.
    - Example: children OR juveniles
- Searching for a term that's commonly associated with a topic you don't want to learn about? Use NOT (or -) in front of the keyword you don't want results from: articles NOT magazines, or: articles – magazines, will bring up results that are about articles, but exclude any results that also include the term magazines.
- Want to get back as many results on a topic as possible? Use * at the end of a word for any letters that might vary: smok*, will bring up results that include the term smoke, smoking, and smokers.

SEARCH ENGINES

Choosing the appropriate search engine for scholarly sources is simple—if one is assigned or you have already become well versed in online research. However, if you are a newbie in the field of research, the following list of electronic search engines may ease some of your research stress.

- College Libraries:
    - The NDSCS Library is called the Mildred Johnson Library. To hit up their search engines, go to ndscs.edu then Library then Resources.
    - Populated by the U.S. Department of Education, the Educational Resources Information Center (ERIC) is a great tool for academic research with more than 1.3 million bibliographic records of articles and online materials.
- Google Scholar was created as a tool to congregate scholarly literature on the web.

STEP 6: HOW DO I CHECK MY SOURCES FOR QUALITY?

OPTION 1: THE CRAAP TEST[150]

The **CRAAP test** is a test to check the reliability of sources across academic disciplines. CRAAP is an acronym for Currency, Relevance, Authority, Accuracy, and Purpose. Due to a vast number of sources existing online, it can be difficult to tell whether these sources are trustworthy to use as tools for research. The CRAAP test aims to make it easier for educators and students to determine if their sources can be trusted. By employing the test while evaluating sources, a researcher can reduce the likelihood of using unreliable information.

- **Currency** means that the information found is the most recent. That said, students and educators may ask where the information was posted or published.

---

[150] Information gathered from *Wikipedia*. This page was last edited on 18 August 2019. Text is available under the Creative Commons Attribution-Share Alike License.

- When looking at sources, the **relevance** of the information will impact a well-rounded research endeavor. One question in this category to ask is how does the topic relate to the information given in a source? More importantly, the writers of the references should focus on the intended audience.
- Student researchers will look to see who the author, publisher, or sponsor is before they can trust the information. Their education level and the author's affiliations are important because this can help the readers know if the author is qualified to write on the topic. There should also be a contact information of the publisher or author.
- The **accuracy** of the contents in the source must connect back to the origin. Evidence must support the information presented to the audience. Evidence can include findings, observations, or field notes. The report must be reviewed or referred. It must be verifiable from another source or common knowledge.
- The questions that arise when looking for the **purpose** range from informing, teaching, selling, entertaining, research or even self-gaining purposes. Also, the author's intentions should be clear. Certain aspects should be taken into consideration whether the information given is fact, opinion, or propaganda as well as political, personal, religious, or ideological bias.

OPTION 2: THE "IF I APPLY" STRATEGY[151]

I – IDENTIFY EMOTIONS ATTACHED TO A TOPIC
i. What are your honest opinions regarding the topic?
ii. Have you addressed your internal biases?
iii. Make an all-inclusive list of counter-opinions or counterarguments.

F - FIND UNBIASED REFERENCE SOURCES THAT WILL PROVIDE A PROPER AND INFORMATIVE OVERVIEW OF THE TOPIC
i. Conduct a general knowledge overview.
ii. Search for information in: encyclopedias, wikis, dictionaries, etc.

I - INTELLECTUAL COURAGE IS NEEDED TO SEEK AUTHORITATIVE VOICES ON THE TOPIC THAT MAY FALL OUTSIDE YOUR COMFORT ZONE OR THESIS
i. Identify credible materials for all the viewpoints - yours and the additional you identified
ii. Reject unsound arguments - have the courage to accept that not all viewpoints are valid

A – AUTHORITY
i. Who is the author (may be individual or organization) and/or publisher?
ii. What are the credentials and affiliation or sponsorship of any named individuals or organizations?
iii. How objective, reliable, and authoritative are they?
iv. Have they written other articles or books?
v. Do they specialize in publishing certain topics or fields?

---

[151] https://libguides.marshall.edu/IFIAPPLY

P – PURPOSE/POINT OF VIEW OF SOURCE
i. Does the author have an agenda beyond education or information?
ii. What can be said about the content, context, style, structure, completeness and accuracy of the information provided by the source?
iii. Are any conclusions offered? If so, based on what evidence and supported by what primary and secondary documentation?
iv. What is implied by the content?
v. Are diverse perspectives represented?
vi. Is the content relevant to your information needs?
vii. Why was the information provided by the source published?
viii. What are the perspectives, opinions, assumptions, and biases of whoever is responsible for this information?
ix. Who is the intended audience?
x. Is anything being sold?

P – PUBLISHER
i. Does the publisher have an agenda?
ii. When was the information published?
iii. Publication date is generally located on the title page or on the reverse side of the title page (copyright date).
iv. Is the information provided by the source in its original form or has it been revised to reflect changes in knowledge?
v. Has the publisher published other works?
vi. Is this information timely and is it updated regularly?
vii. Is the publisher scholarly (university press, scholarly associations)? Commercial? Government agency? Self ("vanity") press?

L – LIST OF RESOURCES
i. Where else can the information provided by the source be found?
ii. Is this information authentic?
iii. Is this information unique or has it been copied?

Y – YEAR OF PUBLICATION
i. What makes information "current" or relevant?
ii. Is this information current? Can you find more current or relevant information?
iii. Is the cited information current? Make sure work is not based on outdated research, statistics, data, etc.
iv. Is the information routinely updated?

STEP 7: HOW DO I CITE SOURCES IN MY TEXT?

Okay, so now you have the research completed and you know which quotes and parts you want to use in your project/paper. And perhaps you have put your sources through the CRAAP test or the "IF I APPLY" strategy, etc. It's time to put the information you found into your project/paper. You'll decide first if you are going to paraphrase or summarize that information, or quote it. After that, you'll figure out how to give credit – with either MLA or APA (or Chicago Style; there are many citation formats).

QUOTATIONS[152]

1. All quoted material should be enclosed in quotations marks unless set off from the rest of the text. Typically, quotes should be 3+ words in a row. If more than 4 lines (MLA) are quoted or 40 words (APA) are quoted, a block quote should be used.

2. Quoted material should be accurate word-for-word. If anything was changed, brackets or ellipsis […] marks should indicated where the changes/omissions took place.

3. A clear signal phrase should alert your readers for each quotation and tell them why the quotation is there. Each quotation must be put in context.

4. A parenthetical citation should follow each quotation.

SUMMARIES (PARAPHRASING)

1. Any summaries of the text should not include plagiarized wording.

2. Summaries must be followed by parenthetical citations.

3. A signal phrase should let your readers know where the summarized material begins as well as tell them why the summary is included in your paper.

STATISTICS & FACTS

1. Any facts that are not common knowledge must have a parenthetical citation included in your paper.

2. Use a signal phrase to help your reader understand why the facts are being cited, unless it is clear enough without one.

MLA AND APA STYLE

Typically, your teacher will require either MLA or APA style (they are the most common). Here are some basics to both styles:

MODERN LANGUAGE ASSOCIATION STYLE

- MLA does not require a title page, asks that the margins be 1" all the way around, requires double-spacing, and sometimes instructors will ask that a student's last name and page number pop up at the top of each page on the right margin after the first page.
- MLA's in-text/parenthetical citations ask for the author's last name, most of all. If that's not available, then throw the article title in there, etc.
- To be considered a block quote (also called long quotations) in MLA, you must have more than four typed lines that you want to quote.

AMERICAN PSYCHOLOGICAL ASSOCIATION STYLE

- APA does recommend a title page, asks that the margins be 1" all the way around, requires double-spacing, and sometimes instructors will ask that a

---

[152] Jeffrey, Robin. *About Writing: A Guide. Revised Edition.* OpenOregon. CC-BY.

student's title pop up in the upper left corner with the page number on the right margin.

- To be considered a block quote (also called long quotations) in APA, you must have more than forty words that you want to quote.

ALSO:

- Indent each paragraph when using MLA or APA style, as well as block quotes (a.k.a. long quotations).
- There is more to these styles – like how to use visuals and headings – so look online or in an updated handbook for more information on those specific writing situations.

This chart uses MLA style.[153]

SITUATION	SAMPLE
Using something word-for-word from another source?	Put quotation marks around the excerpt, use a signal phrase, and include a parenthetical citation with the page number: McGuffin and Cross have said, "No one should ever eat cake without frosting" (22).
Using something word-for-word from another source but changing word forms or adding words to improve clarity and flow?	Put quotation marks around the excerpt, and put brackets around the segments you have changed. Include a signal phrase and a parenthetical citation with the page number: McGuffin and Cross seem to think that "…eat[ing] cake without frosting" should never be allowed (22).
Paraphrasing or summarizing the author's ideas without using the author's exact words?	Use a signal phrase and include a parenthetical citation with the page number: According to McGuffin and Cross, cake is one of those special foods that require an additive to be properly enjoyed, like frosting (22).
Using something from a source but substituting in some synonyms?	PLEASE DON'T. This is plagiarism, even if you use a signal phrase and include a parenthetical citation.

MLA SIGNAL PHRASES
Keep things interesting for your readers by switching up the language and placement of your signal phrases.

- In the words of professors Greer and Dewey, "…"
- As sociology scholar Janice Kinsey has noted, "…"
- Creative Commons, an organization that helps internet users understand and create copyright for materials, reports that "…"
- "…," writes Deidre Tyrell, "…"

---

[153] Jeffrey, Robin. *About Writing: A Guide*. Revised Edition. OpenOregon. CC-BY.

- "…," attorney Sanderson claims.
- Kyles and Sanderson offer up a compelling point: "…"

A FULL PARAGRAPH EXAMPLE USING MLA FORMAT

The definition of the word "controversy" is tough to nail down, sometimes. For me, it's not those people who find ways to push everyone's buttons on a constant basis. No, those people are just mean. Instead, things that are "controversial" to me are things that are more hidden. Eric Haverty covers those people in his online post, but he also had definitions that fit my idea better. For example, he stated that people who "wear clothes reversed and inside out or none at all" are controversial. I agree. He also states that controversial people park where they shouldn't! Keeping with the traveling concept, he also states that controversial people bike wherever they want to, too (Haverty).

This chart uses APA style.

SITUATION	SAMPLE
Using something word-for-word from another source?	Put quotation marks around the excerpt, use a signal phrase, and include a parenthetical citation with the page number, year, and author if not already mentioned: Stephen Hawking (2013) describes the climate at Oxford while he was studying there as "very anti-work" (p. 33). OR The climate at Oxford during his studies is described as "very anti-work" (Hawking, 2013, p. 33).
Using something word-for-word from another source but changing word forms or adding words to improve clarity and flow?	<sample needed>
Paraphrasing or summarizing the author's ideas without using the author's exact words?	Use a signal phrase and include a parenthetical citation with the page number, year, and author if not already mentioned: Stephen Hawking (2013) describes the climate at Oxford while he was studying there (p. 33).
Using something from a source but substituting in some synonyms?	PLEASE DON'T. This is plagiarism, even if you use a signal phrase and include a parenthetical citation.

APA SIGNAL PHRASES
Keep things interesting for your readers by switching up the language and placement of your signal phrases.
- In the words of Peterson (2012), "…"

- As Johnson and Allen (2006) have noted, "…"
- Einstein and Yvanovich (1956), researchers in physics, pointed out that, "…"
- "…," claimed Carter (1998).
- "…," wrote Dietrich (2002), "…"
- Linguists McAllen et al. (2015) have compiled an impressive amount of data for this argument: "…"
- Harrison (2007) answered these criticisms with the following rebuttal: "…"

A FULL PARAGRAPH EXAMPLE USING APA FORMAT

Americans are boastful and Japanese are reserved. These are widely held national stereotypes (Madon et al., 2001), but is there any truth to them? One line of evidence comes from cross-cultural studies of the better-than-average (BTA) effect – people's tendency to judge themselves as better than their peers at a variety of traits and skills (Alicke & Govorun, 2005). The BTA effect tends to be strong and consistent among American participants but weaker and often nonexistent among Japanese participants (Heine, Lehman, Markus, & Kitayama, 1999).

QUESTIONS:

- What might be the citation of the fake source used in "A Full Paragraph Example Using MLA Format"? Use Step 8 to create one.
- What are the full citations of the sources used in "A Full Paragraph Example Using APA Format"?
- What signal phrases – or connecting statements – are used in both full paragraph examples?

STEP 8: HOW DO I CITE SOURCES AT THE END?[154]

Once you begin to wrap up your writing – or this can be done while you are adding to your research paper – you'll create Works Cited Page entries according to the format required. Essentially, you'll want to find all the pieces you can that identify the source you used: author, title, dates, URLs. There are many websites that can assist you in this effort.[155]

WHAT DO YOU NEED FOR A CITATION?[156]

This is a general list of the information you might need to create a complete citation. Depending on the citation style you are using, different information may be required for each of these sources.

FOR BOOKS
• Author(s)
• Editors/translators

---

[154] Most teachers do not expect students to memorize these formats. Just try your best. Use web sites like Easy Bib or Citation Machine if you feel really lost with all of this.

[155] Here is one such website: https://owl.purdue.edu/owl/research_and_citation/resources.html

[156] Jeffrey, Robin. *About Writing: A Guide. Revised Edition.* OpenOregon. CC-BY.

• Edition (if not first)
• Name, date, and city of publication/publisher

MLA Example:
Gleick, James. *Chaos: Making a New Science*. New York, Penguin, 1987.

APA Example:
Gleick, James. (1987). *Chaos: Making a New Science*. New York: Penguin.

FOR ARTICLES
• Author(s)
• Title and Subtitle
• Name of source (magazine, journal, newspaper, etc.)
• Date of publication
• Volume, issue, and page numbers
• Date source retrieved

MLA Example:
Harlow, H.F. "Fundamentals for Preparing Psychology Journal Articles." *Journal of Comparative and Physiological Psychology,* 55, 1983, 893-896.

APA Example:
Harlow, H. F. (1983). Fundamentals for preparing psychology journal articles. *Journal of Comparative and Physiological Psychology, 55*, 893-896.

FOR THE WEB
• Author(s)
• Editors/Creators
• Title of source
• Title of site
• Publication information
• Date of publication or latest update
• Site sponsor
• Date source accessed
• Source URL

Facebook Post:
SAP Books. "It's Officially Live on Amazon." *Facebook*. 30 Nov 21.
https://www.facebook.com/SybilsBooks/posts/336404041625575

Tweet:
Priebe, Sybil. "Create the things you wish existed." *Twitter*. 06 Dec 21.
https://twitter.com/ihaveabug/status/1467800812839649280

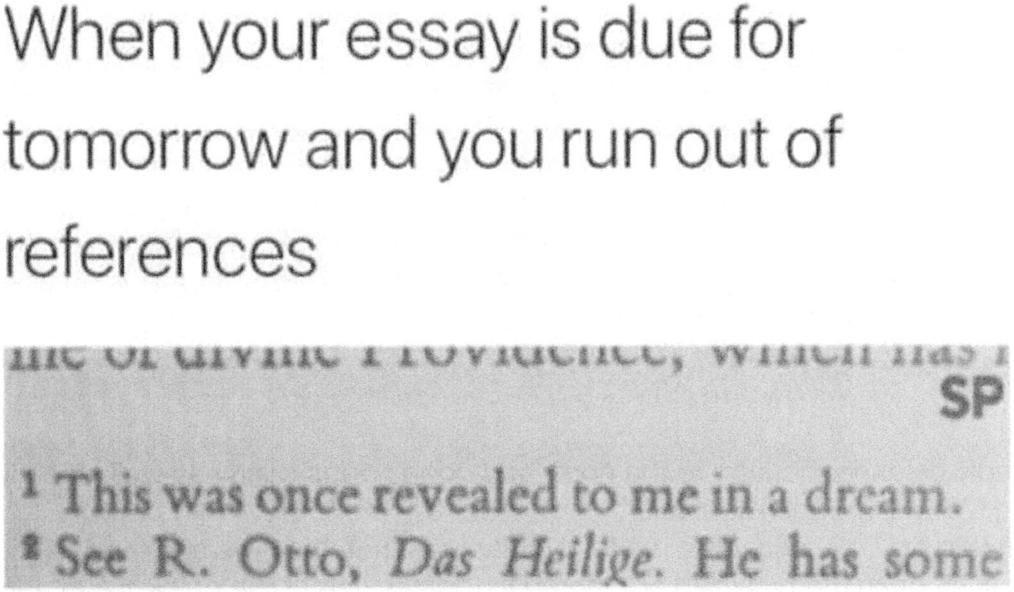

When your essay is due for tomorrow and you run out of references

lie of divine Providence, which has i

SP

¹ This was once revealed to me in a dream.
² See R. Otto, *Das Heilige*. He has some

¹⁵⁷

---

¹⁵⁷ Yes, sometimes using silly footnotes might work!

Student's Name
Teacher's Name
Class Title
06 Nov 2001

The Simpsons and Philosophy: The D'oh of Homer
"Don't you ever, EVER talk that way about television." - Homer Simpson

Is it ONLY a cartoon?

Only in our culture of today would you find such a question. And only in our 21st century way of thinking could you find such an answer.

As many people around the world take in, view, breathe the pop culture that is created and thrown at us on a daily basis by technology, by television, by magazines at a frightening pace, it is hard to take any of it for something more than what we see - what we can suck in from its material presence in front of us. But with an animated show called *The Simpsons* that has proven otherwise.

From the show, a book has evolved. Many college students around the country now own this book, *The Simpsons and Philosophy*. However, it isn't for recreational reading as you may think. It is a required compilation that accompanies other more ancient books in philosophy classes at various universities. In fact, the very man that edited the series the book appears in, *Popular Culture and Philosophy*, is an assistant philosophy professor at Kings College in Pennsylvania.

<<<CONTENT CUT FOR SPACE – CONTENT CUT FOR SPACE>>>

Our friendly neighbor country to the north had good things to say as well. Jason Holt's review in *Canadian Dimension* said[159]:

> In this way, the show is a useful discussion-point. It draws attention to important issues often marginalized or ignored in today's cult of the quick-fix. In addition, it illustrates how, in certain cases, it is ordinary folk, not philosophers, who have gotten things right.

On another note, only one review found the book to be full of itself. Timothy Yenter's review for *RealMagazine.com* of *The Simpsons and Philosophy* said, "Each essay takes a unique approach, and each has its own strengths and weaknesses.... (but) Not all the essays are so successful. Some never deliver the package they claim to offer, or they suffer from oversimplifying philosophical ideas or Simpson characters."

Mainly every reviewer and/or critic had nothing but great hoots and hollers for the book, if not the show as well. It IS a great springboard into philosophy for those not well equipped or versed in the discipline. William Irwin currently uses the book as an incredibly helpful addition to the books required in his class titled: Fundamentals of Philosophy. He, and other philosophy professors from around the United States, find

---

[158] For another student essay example (argument) in both MLA and APA, head to this webpage =
https://roughwritersguide.pressbooks.com/chapter/student-essay-example-1/
[159] This is a block quote, which is used to emphasize information. Typically, one should have THREE sentences' worth of information in a block quote, but this one has two. Oh well. Just breaking some rules over here!

the book an essential contemporary text that allows students and their professors an outlet into a better understanding of how philosophy is interwoven in our American pop culture and daily lives.

It isn't just a cartoon. And it does have many deep meanings. It has influenced us enough to have professors writing essays for a book about it; it has influenced other professors to use it in their very curriculum; it has us talking and laughing about each episode with co-workers, friends, and family. There MUST be more to it then the two-dimensional characters and absurdness that radiates from it into our living rooms. "[It] has managed to be the only consistently funny, consistently smart source of political humor in mainstream American culture," asserted essayist David Kamp in *GQ* magazine ("Satire Still Superior On *The Simpsons*."). Absurdness, yes; satire galore, yes; pop cultural influence in every 30-minute session, yes. And insanely enough, we learn from ourselves more each time we witness Homer and his family living their lives as we do. D'oh!

"Let's go home kids."
"We are home, dad."
"That was fast."

Works Cited

Holt, Jason. Rev. of *The Simpsons and Philosophy*. *Canadian Dimension*. 34.6. (2001): 45.

Kamp, David. "Satire Still Superior on *The Simpsons*." *GQ*. 25 Sept 1998. 11 Oct 2001. <http://www.gq.com/writings/>.

LaCoe, Jean. "*The Simpsons* Give Philosopher Food for Thought." *Times Leader*. 14 Oct 2001. <http://www.timesleader.com/>.

"Simpsons Quotes." *Life Is A Joke.com*. 19 Oct 2001. <http://www.lifeisajoke.com/simpsonspeak/>.

The Official Simpsons Web Site. 10 Oct 2001. <http://www.thesimpsons.com/>.

Yenter, Timothy. Rev. of The Simpsons and Philosophy. *RealMagazine.com*. 14 Oct 2001. <http://www.realmagazine.com/new/>.

*Note: APA Uses a Cover Sheet

The Simpsons and Philosophy: The D'oh of Homer
"Don't you ever, EVER talk that way about television." - Homer Simpson

Is it ONLY a cartoon?

Only in our culture of today would you find such a question. And only in our 21st century way of thinking could you find such an answer.

As many people around the world take in, view, breathe the pop culture that is created and thrown at us on a daily basis by technology, by television, by magazines at a frightening pace, it is hard to take any of it for something more than what we see - what we can suck in from its material presence in front of us. But with an animated show called *The Simpsons* that has proven otherwise.

From the show, a book has evolved. Many college students around the country now own this book, *The Simpsons and Philosophy*. However, it isn't for recreational reading as you may think. It is a required compilation that accompanies other more ancient books in philosophy classes at various universities. In fact, the very man that edited the series the book appears in, *Popular Culture and Philosophy*, is an assistant philosophy professor at Kings College in Pennsylvania.

<<<CONTENT CUT FOR SPACE – CONTENT CUT FOR SPACE>>>

Our friendly neighbor country to the north had good things to say as well. Jason Holt's review in *Canadian Dimension* (2001) said[161]:

> In this way, the show is a useful discussion-point. It draws attention to important issues often marginalized or ignored in today's cult of the quick-fix. In addition, it illustrates how, in certain cases, it is ordinary folk, not philosophers, who have gotten things right.

On another note, only one review found the book to be full of itself. Timothy Yenter's review for *RealMagazine.com* of *The Simpsons and Philosophy* said, "Each essay takes a unique approach, and each has its own strengths and weaknesses.... (but) Not all the essays are so successful. Some never deliver the package they claim to offer, or they suffer from oversimplifying philosophical ideas or Simpson characters" (2001).

Mainly every reviewer and/or critic had nothing but great hoots and hollers for the book, if not the show as well. It IS a great springboard into philosophy for those not well equipped or versed in the discipline. William Irwin currently uses the book as an incredibly helpful addition to the books required in his class titled: Fundamentals of Philosophy. He, and other philosophy professors from around the United States, find the book an essential contemporary text that allows students and their professors an outlet into a better understanding of how philosophy is interwoven in our American pop culture and daily lives.

---

[160] For another student essay example (argument) in both MLA and APA, head to this webpage = https://roughwritersguide.pressbooks.com/chapter/student-essay-example-1/

[161] This is a block quote, which is used to emphasize information. Typically, one should have THREE sentences' worth of information in a block quote, but this one has two. Oh well. Just breaking some rules over here!

It isn't just a cartoon. And it does have many deep meanings. It has influenced us enough to have professors writing essays for a book about it; it has influenced other professors to use it in their very curriculum; it has us talking and laughing about each episode with co-workers, friends, and family. There MUST be more to it then the two-dimensional characters and absurdness that radiates from it into our living rooms. "[It] has managed to be the only consistently funny, consistently smart source of political humor in mainstream American culture," asserted essayist David Kamp in *GQ* magazine ("Satire Still Superior On *The Simpsons*," 1998). Absurdness, yes; satire galore, yes; pop cultural influence in every 30-minute session, yes. And insanely enough, we learn from ourselves more each time we witness Homer and his family living their lives as we do. D'oh!

"Let's go home kids."
"We are home, dad."
"That was fast."

Works Cited

Holt, Jason. (2001) Rev. of *The Simpsons and Philosophy. Canadian Dimension.*

Kamp, David. (1998, Sept. 25). "Satire still superior on *The Simpsons*." GQ.
    Retrieved from http://www.gq.com/writings/.

LaCoe, Jean. (2001, Oct. 14). "*The Simpsons* give philosopher food for
    thought." *Times Leader*. Retrieved from http://www.timesleader.com/>.

"Simpsons quotes." *Life Is A Joke.com*. Retrieved from
    <http://www.lifeisajoke.com/simpsonspeak/>.

The Official Simpsons Web Site. (2001, Oct. 10). Retrieved from
    <http://www.thesimpsons.com/>.

Yenter, Timothy. (2001, Oct. 14) Rev. of *The Simpsons and Philosophy.*
    RealMagazine.com. Retrieved from http://www.realmagazine.com/new/>.

QUESTIONS:
- What's "wrong" with the block quote in these two research paper samples?
- What are the sources used in the research samples? Books? Articles? Web sites? How can you tell by looking at the end citations?

Snopes is a widely respected, non-partisan site dedicated to investigating rumors, memes, social media statements, and news stories and then issuing decisions about whether the materials are correct or false.

Go to *Snopes'* "What's New" page—a page that updates daily and includes the latest rumors: http://www.snopes.com/whats-new/

Scroll through the list until you find an interesting hot topic. Click and read, then write a quick paragraph that summarizes what you found. What did you learn? Were you surprised?

If this captured your interest, you may want to explore *Snopes* a little more. It's a fun place to poke around and a great place to fact-check information.

As humans living in the digital age, we should know how to navigate the Web successfully, find the best materials, and evaluate and use them with confidence. Alas: in an age where a quick Google search nets millions of "hits" in half a second, evaluating the sources we choose can be trickier than it sounds. There's a lot of great material on the Web, but there's a lot of garbage, too. Being able to tell which is which is a digital-age-important life skill.

We also need to understand who "owns" information—whether hard copy (printed) or digital—and how and when to give credit to the owner: this keeps us safe from accidentally committing plagiarism.

Plagiarism occurs when we use someone else's "intellectual property" without giving them credit. Intellectual property is defined as material or ideas envisioned and created by another person. There are many kinds of intellectual property, including books, articles, essays, stories, poems, films, photographs, works of art or craft, or even just ideas. If someone else thought of an idea and brought it into the world, they own it, and if you use their idea in your work, you have to acknowledge them as the actual owner. If you don't? You've committed plagiarism.

QUESTIONS:

- If YOU thought of an idea and brought it into the world, YOU own it. IF someone else uses YOUR idea in their work, they have to acknowledge YOU as the actual owner.
    - How do you feel about this? Does it help you understand the importance of citing someone's work? Why or why not?

---

[162] *The Word on College Reading and Writing* by Carol Burnell, Jaime Wood, Monique Babin, Susan Pesznecker, and Nicole Rosevear is licensed under a Creative Commons Attribution-NonCommercial 4.0 International License, except where otherwise noted.

EXERCISE: FAKE RESEARCH

Create a "Mini-Mock Research Paper" similar to the one below on any topic; you will MAKE UP sources, and quotes. No real research required. In your mock essay, the following is required: Short (direct) quotation, block quote, paraphrase from a source, and a works cited area using the correct format—should include a citation from at least three sources—one interview, one book, and one newspaper or magazine or website article. It's okay if your essay "ends" rather abruptly—you aren't writing the entire essay—just a small chunk of it. No conclusion is necessary. Humor is encouraged and appreciated!

WANT.AN.EXAMPLE?
WANT.A.SAMPLE?

CUCUMBERS ARE GROSS

"A cucumber should be well sliced, and dressed with pepper and vinegar, and then thrown out, as good for nothing" (Johnson). As Samuel Johnson illustrates so clearly in the quote, the cucumber is a disgrace to food everywhere. Studies nationwide have found the cucumber to be the most disliked of all vegetables. In a study I conducted, 90% of respondents said they would never even grow the vegetable in their garden, for fear of its terrible qualities spreading to their other vegetables. Because of its consistency and taste, the cucumber is the grossest food in the human diet.

"One of the most important factors in determining a food's success or failure in popularity is its consistency" (Right 104). Something that tastes slimy when being chewed automatically results in a feeling of disgust. Such is one of the many problems that plagues the cucumber. The interior has a texture like moist fish scales: not hard, but not soft. Doctors Moe, Larry, and Curly explain[163]:

> Basically, the cucumber incorporates water into the construction of its inner and outer skin. In doing so, the hydrocarbons from the cucumber plant only partially bind to one another due to the magnetic interference from the extra water molecules. This partial binding creates the unusual texture experienced when a person bites into a cucumber and adds to the intense flavor. (Fine)

As the good doctors above so clearly articulated, the cucumber's poor texture is a direct result of its own development. The *Center for Steve is Always Right* (CFSAR), in a study contacted last year, found only 6% of Americans didn't mind the gross feel of the cucumber plant. In creating a disgusting surface, it has made its survival much more likely since no one wants to eat something so vile. Or has it? Maybe we should exterminate the horrific plant, but that discussion shall be left for another day. We turn now to the cucumber's taste, another deplorable aspect to an already horrible food.

Works Cited

CFSAR (Center for Steve is Always Right). "Studying the Cucumber's Likeability."

---

[163] THIS is a better example of a block quote because it has three sentences! Woo Whoo!

CFSAR Online. Updated 20 June 2002. Accessed 20 Feb. 2001.
Fine, Dr. Moe; Dr. Larry and Dr. Curly Fine. Personal Interviews. 16 Dec 2001.
Johnson, Samuel L. Personal Interview. 03 April 2001.
Right, Im. *The Culture of Food*. Bismarck: Randomer House, 2001.

QUESTIONS:

- What are the signal phrases – or connection statements to the sources – used in this goofy cucumber sample?
- Where are the following pieces in the fake cucumber sample?
    - Short (direct) quotation?
    - Block quote?
    - A paraphrase from a source?

@Believablee

I can't stand honors college kids. i just asked this girl "hey why aren't koalas considered bears?" and she hits me with "they're marsupials" shut up nerd the answer to the joke is "they don't have the koalafications"

[164]

CHAPTER 7: NERD

Decades of research have shown that isolated grammar exercises[165] are among the worst uses of time in a writing class, given that such practices can result in students' writing actually getting worse.[166] Education researchers did a meta-analysis (a compilation, summary, and recommendation) of many research projects on writing over the years. In their 2007 report to the Carnegie Corporation of New York, Steve Graham and Dolores Perin found that isolated (traditional) grammar teaching was the only instructional practice to actually have a negative[167]—that's right, negative— impact on students' writing. In the 1980s, George Hillocks, Jr. conducted a comprehensive synthesis of writing research that went back to studies done in the

---

[164] This tweet is currently from a suspended account; it might've been deleted?

[165] Snippet from = Dunn, Patricia A. "Teaching Grammar Improves Writing." *Bad Ideas About Writing*. Edited by Cheryl E. Ball and Drew M. Loewe. Morgantown, WV: West Virginia University Libraries, Digital Publishing Institute, 2017. CC-BY.

[166] Oh my god!

[167] Yikes!

early 1960s. Hillocks's academic article, "Synthesis of Research on Teaching Writing," and his book, Research on Written Composition, could not have been clearer about the harmful[168] effects of traditional grammar.

However, a technique called sentence combining (where students take a series of short sentences and combine them into longer ones, using a mix of clauses, phrases, and linking punctuation) did fairly well in multiple studies of student writing.[169] In other words, students who did sentence combining (crafting short sentences into longer ones, actively manipulating sections of sentences,[170] rearranging clauses and phrases, adding or deleting modifying words, and punctuating the longer sentence so that it was smooth) saw their own writing improve after this work. But grammar exercises—quizzes[171] on parts of speech, the naming of types of phrases, clauses, and sentences? After those, students' writing got worse.

But no one believes this research—other than those who conduct or study writing as a career. So convinced is the general public that young writers are in desperate need of old-fashioned, rigorous grammar, that writing teachers from grade school through grad school continue to be pressured to teach grammar as a way to improve writing. Even some teachers continue to think that if only grammar could be drilled into students in a fun, engaging way, students would write correctly[172] ever after. It doesn't happen.[173]

+

It goes without saying that everyone appreciates clear, well-edited writing. But teaching grammar won't help because clarity is slippery.[174] What's clear to one reader might be unclear to the next, depending on his or her respective background knowledge. For example, sewing directions would be clear to a tailor, but not to someone who has never picked up a needle and thread. An article in a physics journal would be clear to a physicist, but not to a pharmacist.

Even what is considered so-called correct writing can vary depending on the conventions expected in a particular genre or publication. (Google "Oxford comma" if you want to see sparks fly over conflicting views of punctuation[175].) Every writing project is constrained by previous iterations of that type of writing. Is it a memo, résumé, game manual, business plan, film review? Its context and publication also shapes its readers' expectations. A letter to the editor of *The New York Times* has some features in common with a letter to the editor of *Newsday* (a local Long Island paper), but even this same genre looks different in these two publications. Everything from punctuation to evidence presented in the respective letters is noticeably different, including sentence structure and length, vocabulary level, and rhetorical appeals aimed at different readerships.

---

[168] Sad face.

[169] Huh. Maybe we should only focus on those activities, then?

[170] Cool, so let's add those kinds of activities to this chapter, right?

[171] No quizzes in this book on those items – just helpful AND OPTIONAL review!

[172] This word should be in quotation marks.

[173] Agreed. It won't happen in this book.

[174] You'll see a lot of slippery ideas in this chapter.

[175] Do you know what an Oxford comma is? Go ahead and Google it to see what the controversy is all about. Or read the upcoming piece called "The Comma Comma."

- o Why do YOU think "no one believes this research"?
- o Do you understand the idea that "clarity is slippery?" Can you think of your own example beyond the example above that compares a physicist to a pharmacist?

STYLE

You may see the term "style"[176] scattered throughout your writing courses. The term is little bit complex. Here are a few things you might be asked to look for as you revise for academic style:

- Academic (formal) tone—no "you" or "one" because these pronouns are broad and vague (but "I/we" are fine)
- Appropriate language
- Clichés and colloquial language
- Sentence variety (simple, compound, complex)
- Author voice
- Active vs. passive construction
  - *I wrote the paper. YES!*
  - *The paper was written by me. NO!*

These are excellent suggestions, but certain phrases such as "appropriate" vs. "colloquial" language raise the question of what's suitable for an academic audience. These expectations are often interpreted to mean that students should practice "standard American English." All other non-standard dialects, such as Black English or certain types of Southern slang, are viewed as inappropriate because they're "lesser than" the standard.[177] This is why revising or editing in the name of style is… complex.

Writing for an academic audience does often mean students will sound more formal and less like everyday speech, but it's a mistake to view the latter, non-standard forms of writing and speech as lesser than academic communication.

---

[176] This snippet is from "Style and Linguistic Diversity" in *Write What Matters*. *Write What Matters* by Liza Long; Amy Minervini; and Joel Gladd is licensed under a Creative Commons Attribution-NonCommercial-ShareAlike 4.0 International License, except where otherwise noted.
[177] Remember the chapter on White People Language? Yeah.

FIGURATIVE LANGUAGE

THE ENGLISH LANGUAGE IS WEIRD.[178]

This chapter exists for those students and teachers who wish to dig a little deeper into the English language because it's a weird language. In our weird language, we have words and phrases that don't always follow their normal meaning… yeah, imagine that! So, not only do we have slang words and phrases evolving at a wild rate – while also getting created by people weekly – this category is full of words and phrases that can change the meaning of a sentence without trying very hard.

There are few ways to use figurative language, including metaphors, similes, personification, and hyperbole. There is a lot to the category of figurative language; this chapter might not cover ALL of them, but here's a start:

DOUBLE ENTENDRES

When a sentence means something literally while also meaning something perverted at the same time.
- Mateo grabbed his ball before hitting it over the net.

EUPHEMISMS

When a person wants to discuss a taboo topic but uses a socially known code to talk about it. We seem to have a lot of euphemisms when it comes to sex and our digestive systems.
- Malik urgently scooted to the bathroom; he had a call on line two.
- Joe and Tae got nasty in the backseat of the Jeep.

OXYMORONS

A phrase with contradicting terms side by side.
- Small elephant
- Jumbo shrimp

CLICHÉS

These are "overused"[179] phrases. Sometimes, they are okay to use; sometimes, they annoy your readers.
- Isabella's personality is wild; she's like a chicken with its head chopped off.
- I found out my teacher is an ungrader; it is the cherry on top of my day!

HYPERBOLE

These are incredible exaggerations.
- Ria's hair was so tall it reached the sky.

---

[178] This chapter is brought to you by Sybil Priebe.
[179] According to whom, I don't know.

- Derek's wheelchair was faster than a car.

PERSONIFICATION

This occurs when we give humanistic characteristics to non-humans.
- The grocery cart was acting like a jerk.
- At the top of my cane is a bump; it's like a pimple.

METAPHORS & SIMILES

These are used in comparisons.
- Malik is as weird as Ria is. Ria is like an antenna for weirdness.

PUNS

The best explanation of this term might be to just say: "Corny jokes that older people tell."
- Malik shook the lettuce in my face and said, "Romaine calm!"

ALLITERATION

When the same consonants keep popping up in a sentence or poem.
- Sally sells seashells by the seashore.

ONOMATOPOEIA

This term is used when a word sounds like the sound it makes.
- "Pop" went the champagne; it was time to celebrate the Pride parade!

IDIOM

These are common phrases, that unlike clichés, are sometimes considered words of wisdom. Some claim they are big ideas condensed down into tiny bits.
- a little bird told me / a drop in the bucket / a bitter pill / a man of few words

FIGURATIVE LANGUAGE EXERCISES:

EXERCISE 1:
In a 250-500 worded story about anything, use the following types of figurative language: 10+ Euphemisms. Underline the euphemisms.

EXERCISE 2:
In a 250-500 worded story about anything, use the following types of figurative language: 10+ Double Entendres. Underline the double entendres.

EXERCISE 3:
In a 250-500 worded story about anything, use the following types of figurative language: 5 Similes/Metaphors and 5 Oxymorons. Underline the similes (and/or metaphors) and put oxymorons in italics.

EXERCISE 4:
The Combo Challenge – Complete all three activities above in ONE essay/story!

EXERCISE 5:
Create your own figurative language activity and complete it or exchange it with a classmate.

ENGLISH IS A DIFFICULT LANGUAGE.
IT CAN BE UNDERSTOOD
THROUGH TOUGH THOROUGH
THOUGHT, THOUGH.

WHY IS ENGLISH SO MUCH FUN?

" ALL THE FAITH HE HAD HAD HAD HAD NO EFFECT ON THE OUTCOME OF HIS LIFE. "

BECAUSE THAT SENTENCE MAKES PERFECT SENSE.

CHAPTER 8: WHAT'S NEXT?

Congratulations![180] You've done it. You've reached the end of this book, and hopefully you know more about writing than you did when you started.

If this textbook has done its job well, it's answered many of your questions, helped you come up with new ones, given you a toolbox of fresh skills, and broadened your exposure to writing. And you? You've put hours of time and practice into becoming a stronger writer, and you've reaped the benefits and pride of those efforts. Well done!

So, what's next? How can you keep polishing and using your new writing skills? Here are a few suggestions:

---

[180] *The Word on College Reading and Writing* by Carol Burnell, Jaime Wood, Monique Babin, Susan Pesznecker, and Nicole Rosevear is licensed under a Creative Commons Attribution-NonCommercial 4.0 International License, except where otherwise noted.

- First and foremost, write! Try to write a little every day. Many writers accomplish this by keeping a journal or diary.
- Keep your writing skills fine-tuned by reading articles (online or in a hard copy newspaper or magazine) and then writing quick summaries or even short essays in which you respond to or argue with the articles. Doing this will keep your skills sharp.
- Push yourself even more by creating a blog or social media site where you can post some of your writing or create a daily paragraph or two about a favorite topic. Making your writing available publicly is a big step and will boost your growing confidence.
- Write letters to friends and family members and companies. They'll love receiving them, and you may even get a reply.
- And,[181] this is very important: READ. Read something every day, whether a newspaper story, blog post, magazine article, or a favorite book. Being a good reader will help strengthen your writing skills through exposure to all sorts of ideas, essay structures, and language use.

Like any other skill set, your writing will improve, become easier, and increasingly enjoyable with practice. Here's wishing you continued growth and even more pride as you move further into the world of writing!

---

[181] No idea why there is a comma here.

END ON A SILLY NOTE

Things I Wish I Knew When I Was 16, according to former students at NDSCS

//Motorcycles save a lot on gas. Don't quit a sport to work; be smart about it. Don't eat McDonalds every day. Spend more time with your mom. Have a good rapport with the janitors and the lunch ladies. You don't have to be the best-looking guy to get a girl – usually making them laugh is a great place to start. Go to bed as early as possible. I wish I knew that the amount of girls you had sex with doesn't help you get a job promotion. Don't worry about not growing a beard; it doesn't make you any more of a man. Don't worry about how much alcohol you can consume, unless you want to spend big bucks on booze. Your vehicle doesn't have to be super awesome or new as long as it gets you from point A to B. Your mom won't always be there to do your laundry or make your appointments. Common courtesy is a huge factor in how you get treated and respected: Please/Thank you! Friends and acquaintances are easily mixed up at such a young age. Use your voice. Wear a condom. The cute ones are usually the worst ones. Let the haters hate. Don't be intimidated by college: kick its ass. Stop trying to impress people. It's never late to do the right thing. Trust needs to be earned. Alcohol abuse will give you the illusion of happiness. Lasting and true beauty is within. My teachers aren't out to make my life hell. Being a leader is a cursing and a blessing. You can make it out of the hood. A lot of people are fake. Stay true to who you are. Enjoy youth. Making excuses gets you nowhere. Help anyone in need. Work for what you want - no cutting corners or kissing asses. Always wear your seat belt. To brush my teeth all the time like the orthodontist said to. Don't be a little prick to people even if you don't care for them. That chewing tobacco isn't cool. Learn how to speak a different language. How to ask for a raise and how to start a business. To be more open to everything. Learn how to play an instrument. It's okay to save sex for marriage. Never play a game of pick-up basketball in expensive jeans. Speeding tickets are expensive. Car payments are hell. No one is perfect. Hormones suck! Wearing make-up is not a must. There are more fish in the sea. Have something to live for (figure out your purpose in life). You are an amazing person. Change a diaper. Underwear lines don't matter. It's okay to be alone. Cheating is only cheating yourself. Give people a second chance. You're not FAT. Don't follow the family tradition. Life is short so you have to say F*CK it every now and then. Don't drop college algebra. Buy more guns. Take time to slow down. Drugs are bad, mmkay? Learn how to drive a stick.//

RESOURCES

- A Google folder of all things open/OER, including this textbook (in different formats): bit.ly/NDSCS-Open-Folder
- A Google folder of all things related to Ungrading: bit.ly/sybil_ungrading

+

ABOUT THE AUTHOR

Sybil Priebe lives in the upper Midwest and teaches at a community & technical college in southeastern North Dakota. She likes books, bicycles, and blasphemy. You can find her at: sybilannpriebe@gmail.com

Made in United States
North Haven, CT
29 August 2023

40898024R00109